# WHAT
# VEGANS
# EAT

# WHAT VEGANS EAT

## BRETT COBLEY

HarperCollins*Publishers*

HarperCollins*Publishers*
1 London Bridge Street
London SE1 9GF

www.harpercollins.co.uk

First published by HarperCollins*Publishers* 2018

1 3 5 7 9 10 8 6 4 2

Text © Brett Cobley 2018

Photography © Andrew Burton 2018

Brett Cobley asserts the moral right to be identified
as the author of this work

A catalogue record of this book is available from the British Library

ISBN 978-0-00-832079-9

Food styling: Emily Jonzen
Prop styling: Alexander Breeze

Printed and bound by GPS

MIX
Paper from
responsible sources
FSC
www.fsc.org
FSC™ C007454

FSC™ is a non-profit international organisation established to promote
the responsible management of the world's forests. Products carrying the
FSC label are independently certified to assure consumers that they come
from forests that are managed to meet the social, economic and
ecological needs of present and future generations,
and other controlled sources.

Find out more about HarperCollins and the environment at
**www.harpercollins.co.uk/green**

*The process of writing this book has been incredibly rewarding and enjoyable. It also took a huge amount of time and energy, so I would like to dedicate this book to all my friends and family for the amazing love and support I received throughout this process!*

*I would also like to say a big thanks to the team of people that worked on this book for their hard work and expertise. Without the individual strengths of a team working together, success is never possible.*

---

# CONTENTS

# Why write this book?

'What do vegans eat?' This is a question that every vegan has been asked multiple times, or one that is often pondered by those yet to take the vegan plunge. There have even been songs written about it! But in this book I hope I've answered that question once and for all, with delicious, no-nonsense, simple and realistic recipes that are tasty and satisfying.

You might have friends who follow a vegetarian diet, which excludes meat, poultry and fish but usually includes eggs and dairy, but not realise that a vegan diet is more discerning when it comes to animal welfare. A vegan diet rules out all foods that derive from animals in any form, including dairy products, eggs, gelatine and honey.

There are so many reasons to go vegan – and amazing food is a big one! Discovering incredible flavours through simple ingredients, getting creative with your cooking and sharing the love of good food with family and friends is

so rewarding. On top of this, you'll be effortlessly showing compassion for animals and respect for other living creatures, while also experiencing the health benefits of cutting meat and dairy from our diets that have been proven time and again. The impact of animal agriculture on our environment – from deforestation, to the use of fishing nets – is one of the reasons why I am, and always will be, vegan. However, your diet and lifestyle is a very personal choice. So, no matter where you are in your journey to veganism, I hope that this will be the book that helps you cook with confidence and creativity for yourself as well as friends and family, and ultimately encourage you to ponder, why did I ever eat any other way?

Make sure you visit my Instagram page @epivegan, for lots more recipe photos including all the recipes you'll find in this book!

## Top tips for new vegans

When doing anything new it can feel like there is a lot of pressure to get it right first time, and this can lead to negative thinking about the journey to reaching that goal, where one slip-up might lead to giving up. Adopting a vegan diet can take time as you learn more about what's in your food and you explore new ingredients. So don't panic – simply take care, read the labels, ask what something contains if you're not sure, but, most importantly, if you find you've eaten something and realised afterwards that it wasn't vegan, do not despair and don't give up!

Here are a few of my top tips so you won't get caught out:

• Look out for milk. One of the most common issues when grabbing lunch or a snack on the go, or doing your weekly shop is that so many things contain hidden milk. This is most prominent in things like snacks: crisps commonly have milk powder in the flavouring, occasionally even in salt and vinegar flavours. Milk is also often hidden by its different names, so watch out for anything with lactic or whey in the name.

• Anti-caking agents can also crop up in unexpected places, and these often contain animal bone – they are called things like 'bone phosphate'.

The following ingredients are never vegan, so check for these:

ALBUMEN - an egg white protein.

BEESWAX - comes from bees, obviously!

CASEIN - a protein obtained from dairy.

COCHINEAL (CARMINE) - is a dye made from acid extracted from female insects.

CONFECTIONER'S GLAZE - uses shellac, which is made from beetle cocoons.

FOOD-GRADE WAX - often from beeswax, and therefore bees.

GELATINE - jellified animal fats, often used as a gelling agent in food.

ISINGLASS - a gelatine obtained from fish.

LARD - animal fat.

RENNET - this is used in cheesemaking and comes from milk.

VITAMIN D3 - often comes from fish, beef liver or eggs (unless specified as a vegan alternative).

WHEY - a protein from milk.

# Pantry essentials

### NUTRITIONAL YEAST

A pantry must-have! Available in most supermarkets, health food stores and online. Nutritional yeast has a cheesy, nutty taste and is a great source of B vitamins, including B12, which is often referred to as a hard-to-get vitamin in the vegan diet. It contains antioxidants and has been proven to lower cholesterol, but another great factor is the amount of protein it contains – 9g per serving, which is 20 per cent of most people's recommended intake.

GOOD FOR: Thickening sauces and adding a slightly cheesy taste!

### VEGAN CREAM

This is a great addition to the pantry and is widely sold in all major supermarkets by brands such as Alpro as soy cream, and Oatly as oat cream.

GOOD FOR: Soy cream is perfect for creamy pasta sauces or for pouring over a tasty steaming dessert. It's a great alternative to single cream; it can't be whipped like a double cream; but that's where coconut cream comes in!

### TOFU

Great to have in the cupboard or fridge. The silken version usually comes in a tetra pack; it's long-life and doesn't require refrigeration, while firm tofu comes in a block packed with water, either plain, flavoured with spices or smoked.

GOOD FOR: Silken tofu is amazing for recreating egg-style dishes and creamy sauces. Firm tofu is perfect for cubing, slicing, marinating and baking or frying.

### TINNED CHICKPEAS

I've saved the best to last. Chickpeas are unbeatable for versatility and they are the perfect pulse to fill you up!

GOOD FOR: Always have chickpeas handy and remember to save the juice, or aquafaba as it's known, for making mayonnaise, meringues, omelettes and so much more. The chickpeas themselves can be used in vegan tuna, hummus and koftes.

## SPILL THE BEANS

Beans and pulses are a pantry staple as they are an excellent protein source.

GOOD FOR: Everything from a mince replacement to cooking up minestrones or beans on toast, they are the perfect addition to any dish when you want an extra boost of fibre and protein. The types I always have to hand in tins are:

### HARICOT BEANS

GOOD FOR: You'll be most familiar with these as those in the classic tin of baked beans. Perfect for creating your own beans on toast or served in a BBQ sauce.

### GREEN LENTILS

GOOD FOR: Replacing minced meat in cottage pie, Bolognese or simply adding to a dish as a protein-boosting side. Plus they are quick to cook, and if bought tinned they are even quicker!

### RED LENTILS

GOOD FOR: A curry or dhal dish and ideal when you want to make a cheap, satisfying, wholesome meal.

### KIDNEY BEANS

GOOD FOR: You'll have undoubtedly been using these nutritionally packed beans in your chillies already. They are also great for making spicy bean spreads or adding to tacos.

### BUTTER BEANS

The only 'butter' you'll ever really need! Perhaps the heartiest of all the beans.

GOOD FOR: Perfect for taking on flavour, these are generally big beans and are really satisfying to bake or add to a minestrone as they have an almost creamy texture.

# Flavour makers

Regardless of your diet, every pantry needs to contain some serious flavour makers. The very basics for every spice cupboard include:

### BASIL

Dried basil has a completely different flavour to fresh, and in some situations it is no substitute. However, for those times when you need to fry something and want a basil flavour, the dried version really comes into its own.

### CINNAMON

The sticks aren't something I would recommend you make space for in your cupboard; although they look great in a fancy photo or if you're making mulled wine, ground cinnamon is the real star. You can add it to cakes and sprinkle it on sweet treats, of course, but it is also lovely with root vegetables, perfectly complementing their sweetness and adding a little warming spice.

### CUMIN

A curry is barely a curry without it. Cumin is a real all-round performer when it comes to adding flavour to spicy dishes. Keep it handy.

### CURRY POWDER

This is a must for adding sweetness and spice to curried dishes such as dhals. Great for making your own curry sauces or experimenting with curried hummus.

### GARAM MASALA

This hot masala blend is used in curry dishes. It has a fantastic depth of flavour with some heat that means a little goes a long way.

### GARLIC POWDER

Powerful and tasty, but be careful not to overdo it as it can quickly overpower a dish. A little goes a very long way as it is packed with flavour.

### LEMON

Citrus flavour from fresh lemons is great when used in baking or in traditionally Asian, Italian or Mexican dishes, being both tangy and sweet. Use sparingly, as it is powerful; citrus flavours should be used to complement a dish but add too much and you will quickly overpower other flavours.

### LIME

This fruit is used in a lot of traditional Mexican dishes for its strong flavour, but also as a preservative, because its acidity extends the life of rapid perishables like guacamole. Lime is also used to offset the heat of many dishes with its tangy fresh taste. Keep both lemons and limes handy to balance flavours and extend the life of perishables.

### MAPLE SYRUP

This is a real staple of my pantry cupboard. Maple syrup is incredibly diverse; it's great in salad dressings as well as baking, or to add sweetness to a dish and offset the spice or salt taste. Of course it doesn't hurt that it is also amazing on pancakes, waffles and French toast.

### MUSTARD SEEDS

These little seeds give a good punch of heat and flavour, which is why I've used them in my chickpea curry (see page 110). Try using mustard seeds to create your own maple mustard sauce – it will leave you wondering why you ever used honey.

### NUTMEG

Once grated this is great for baking, and also as a sprinkled topping. Nutmeg has a subtle sweetness and spice that makes it great to pair with rice pudding, porridge and cakes. It might not be your go-to spice, but it is worth keeping around as a flavour-making finishing touch.

### ONION POWDER

Does what it says on the tin – onion powder is an intense onion flavour for when you really want a deep onion flavour, but to add more onions would leave the dish unbalanced.

### OREGANO

Dried oregano is very diverse but is traditionally used in Italian dishes. Pair this with smoked paprika, onion salt and a little garlic powder and use it to season potatoes, then thank me later.

### PARSLEY

This leaf is potentially one of the most useful herbs in the kitchen. Parsley has a fresh aroma and earthy flavour. Freshly chopped on top of a minestrone or casserole, it is just the ticket.

## PEPPER

Freshly ground black pepper is a must when topping salads, pasta or bean dishes and is also great for creating gravies and sauces, while white peppercorns are useful for adding punch to dishes like the Thai green greens (see page 138).

## ROSEMARY

Traditionally paired with root veg, combining sea salt with rosemary really gets the flavour going. The strong scent of this herb adds to its power.

## SALT

We all know that salt is a chief flavour maker, but it is not as basic as it seems. Smoked sea salt can completely change the game when it comes to savoury cooking and if you have the extra space in your cupboards or racks, garlic or onion salts are always a great addition, however they are not a necessity.

## SMOKED PAPRIKA (FLAKES AND GROUND)

A fantastic spice with a very complementary depth of flavour. Those who know the wonders of smoked paprika will spice and sprinkle a lot of their food with it.

## THYME

A great dried herb to have in the herb and spice rack. It's perfect for seasoning potatoes in any form and adds a subtle, aromatic twist to breads and baking.

## TURMERIC

This wizard is not just for adding flavour to your curry or making a fancy latte. Turmeric is also a powerful antioxidant and acts as an anti-inflammatory. It is recommended that you eat it in some form every single day, and it is more active when combined with black pepper. It's taken by many athletes in pill form purely for its inflammation-reducing properties.

# Plant milks

Fortified plant milks are such an asset to the vegan diet. There are so many types and they can be used for a variety of purposes. I've given my preferred plant-based milk in particular recipes, but feel free to mix it up. If you're overwhelmed by the choice, here are a few tips to decide which milk fits your needs.

SOY OR 'SOYA' MILK
This is probably the most well-known plant-based milk, and one that is widely available. Part of the reason for this is that it has a very long shelf life and can be used in baking, hot and cold drinks, and also on cereal. It isn't the creamiest or most luxurious option, but it can be just the trick when you are looking for a gluten- and nut-free milk.

GOOD FOR: An all-rounder and a good alternative for those who can't have nuts – fine for hot and cold drinks and baking.

CASHEW MILK
This is one of my favourite milks! It is creamy and tastes great. It's perfect in coffee or in baking as well as being great for thickening to make any dish extra saucy. This creamy, delicious milk is a really useful ingredient, but do check if people have nut allergies before serving to others.

GOOD FOR: Hot drinks and baking.

OAT MILK
Although not gluten free, this milk is rich and creamy. Oatly Barista milk is one of the best possible brands for hot drinks as it combines perfectly without separation.

GOOD FOR: Barista-style hot drinks, especially milky coffee.

**RICE MILK**   Creamy, delicious and tasty. Rice milk is great for cereals and can be used for baking, too. Not as diverse as some of the thicker milks, but it is often sweetened and can be rather tasty with vanilla.

GOOD FOR: Baking, porridge and other cereals.

**COCONUT MILK**   Traditionally sold in tins for use in cooking to give a creaminess to a curry or help calm the heat of a dish. But there are also versions sold as plant milks for cereal and drinks if you like the coconutty taste.

GOOD FOR: Savoury dishes such as soups and curries.

**HEMP MILK**   Available in most major supermarkets, this is a winner! Hemp milk ticks a lot of boxes as it is high in protein and great in a protein shake or with cereal or drinks.

GOOD FOR: Shakes and cereals.

**ALMOND MILK**   This is the go-to for hot drinks for many people, but it does alter the flavour quite significantly – it can taste sweet to some, bitter to others. Personally, I think almond milk is a bit too thin for coffee, but it can work well in baking. Again, be sure to check for allergies before serving it to others.

GOOD FOR: Baking, cereal and some hot drinks, but the consistency can vary.

# Bases and basics

FLOUR
Always useful in all kinds of baking, this is a traditional staple and forms the base of countless recipes. Self-raising is incredibly useful in vegan recipes for its additional rising properties, which are required when eggs are removed. I always recommend using unbleached flours whenever possible as bleaching is unnecessary and is bad for gut health.

CORNFLOUR
An excellent thickening agent to help turn thinner plant milks into a thicker creamy sauce when vegan creams aren't to hand.

ARROWROOT
Great for thickening and setting, this is used in the vegan omelette recipe in this book (see page 35). Arrowroot also has beneficial properties for treating stomach issues and even improving the skin.

BAKING POWDER
A great raising agent used for replacing eggs in vegan cakes and baked goods.

BICARBONATE OF SODA
Great for adding air to spongy recipes when combined with acidic ingredients like apple cider vinegar.

FLAXSEEDS
These amazing little seeds are great for digestion as they are a good source of fibre. They can also be ground and combined with water to be used as a binding agent when creating balls or patties, to replace egg whites.

APPLE CIDER VINEGAR
Not only great for dressing salads and for its medicinal properties, but also often combined with bicarbonate of soda to create a fizz and replace eggs when baking.

# Where's your protein?

Where do you get your protein from? Did you ever hear that question before you went vegan, thought about going vegan or looked into it at all? Did you ever worry about it? No? Good, you still don't need to – even on a vegan diet. The protein consumed by animals that is transferred to those eating meat comes from the abundance of proteins in the plant world. We've all heard the sound bites such as broccoli containing more protein per calorie than steak, and there is no smoke without fire, but the truth is we don't need these facts and figures to prove we are getting enough goodness from our food. Animal proteins are 'complete' proteins, as they contain all the essential amino acids your body needs. Plant proteins are incomplete, lacking one or more amino acid, so you need to combine sources of different amino acids to get everything your body needs. If you have a balanced, varied diet, protein deficiency is not something you will likely ever suffer from, with or without animal products. A main reason why people can suffer from a protein deficiency is due to issues with absorption of nutrients, which is something that must be addressed, regardless of your chosen diet.

However, if you are embarking on a meat- and dairy-free diet for the first time and are still concerned, or want to get some extra protein in for a long day or pre- or post-workout, here are some great sources that can be added to pretty much any dish:

- QUINOA
- BUCKWHEAT
- SOY AND TOFU
- BROWN RICE
- BEANS AND LENTILS (SEE PAGE 13)
- NUTS AND NUT MILK
- OATS
- SEITAN
- TEMPEH
- SPIRULINA
- HEMP SEEDS
- PEAS AND OTHER LEGUMES
- CHIA SEEDS
- LOTS OF VEGETABLES, BUT THE REAL PROTEIN HEROES ARE BROCCOLI, KALE, SPINACH, SPROUTS AND MUSHROOMS
- HIGH-PROTEIN BREAD- such as Ezekiel Bread – a type of sprouted bread made from whole grains and legumes that have begun to 'sprout'. Compared to white bread, made with refined wheat flour, Ezekiel bread is much richer in nutrients and fibre, with no added sugar.

# 01

# What Vegans Eat

—

# Every Day

# FOR
# BREAKFAST

## BREAKFAST EVERY DAY

Pancakes

PB&J soaked oats

Chia pudding

Quinoa and apple porridge

Dirty beans on toast

Chocolate orange chia pudding

---

## STEALING THE SHOW

Apple and cinnamon French toast

Vegan omelette

Benedict of the doubt

Pancakes are always a crowd-pleaser. Whether you like them stacked up high, served traditionally with sugar and lemon, or covered in all kinds of peanut butter or chocolate decadence, these light and fluffy pancakes are for you. These are the American-style versions, which are ideal for making in small, puffy discs.

# Pancakes

SERVES 4

150g (1¼ cups) plain flour
1 tsp baking powder
250ml (1 cup) almond milk
   or rice milk
2 tbsp maple syrup
1 tsp vanilla extract
Pinch of salt
Oil, for frying

Combine the flour and baking powder in a large bowl, then add all the remaining ingredients, except the oil, and mix together with a whisk. You aren't trying to whisk the mixture or add bubbles here, but a whisk just works best to make the batter nice and smooth.

Use a brush to apply a thin layer oil to a frying pan set over a low heat, then add 1 tablespoon of the batter mixture to the pan – keeping it flat and level to make a neat circular pancake. Cook for a little over 30 seconds until the pancake is firm enough to slide when you shake the pan, then flip it over and cook for another 30 seconds until both sides are crispy and golden. Keep the pancake somewhere warm while you make the others. Cook the rest of the batter in the same way – you should have between 12 and 16 pancakes.

Serve with your preferred toppings – my favourite way to serve these beauties is with coconut cream and fresh strawberries.

Peanut butter and jelly/jam is a classic flavour combination that has stood the test of time. Why not get some soaked oats involved and have a really tasty breakfast to start your day off right? Feel free to mix things up using different types of nut butters, berries and plant-based milks to customise this dish.

## PB&J soaked oats

SERVES 2

75g (¾ cup) rolled oats

1 banana, sliced

115g (½ cup) frozen pitted cherries (or use your favourite berry, such as strawberry)

2 tbsp of your favourite nut butter

250ml (1 cup) hemp or oat milk

Add the oats to a large jar or a bowl followed by the sliced banana, cherries or berries and finally the nut butter. Make sure the nut butter isn't creating a barrier between the milk and the oats, then pour the milk into the jar or bowl so that it coats the oats. Seal the jar or cover the bowl, then leave in the fridge for anywhere between 1 hour and overnight.

Remove from the fridge 30 minutes before you want to eat it to allow the oats to reach room temperature. Enjoy!

Chia pudding is a nutritious and wholesome breakfast that is right on trend. These amazing little seeds soak up the plant-based milk and puff up to create a delicious rice pudding-like consistency.

# Chia pudding

SERVES 2

Handful of your favourite berries, plus extra to serve
40g (⅓ cup) chia seeds
½ tsp grated nutmeg
½ tsp ground cinnamon
1 tsp vanilla extract
Pinch of Himalayan salt
1 tbsp maple syrup
375ml (1½ cups) cashew milk

Combine the berries and chia seeds in a small bowl.

Whisk together the nutmeg, cinnamon, vanilla extract, salt, maple syrup and milk in a jug, then pour over the seeds and berries and stir gently to combine. Cover the bowl and leave in the fridge overnight to set.

Serve the next morning with a few berries on top.

Worried about getting enough protein? Why not include quinoa in your breakfast? Quinoa is a complete protein with a full amino-acid profile, which means your body can utilise it really well. This porridge is perfect for a cold morning – comforting, warm and tasty, and it will fill you up and keep you going for hours.

# Quinoa and apple porridge

SERVES 2

50g (¼ cup) quinoa, rinsed and drained
25g (¼ cup) rolled oats
½ teaspoon ground cinnamon
1 apple, peeled, cored and grated
40g (¼ cup) raisins
1 tbsp ground flaxseed
125ml (½ cup) cashew milk or coconut milk

*To serve (optional)*
1 tsp chia seeds
Handful of raisins
Maple syrup
Coconut milk
Nuts, seeds, etc.

Add the quinoa and oats to a small pan along with the cinnamon. Pour in 125ml (½ cup) water and bring to the boil, then lower the heat and simmer for 10 minutes.

Stir in the grated apple, raisins and ground flaxseed, then pour in the milk, stir and leave to simmer for another 10 minutes.

Serve the porridge immediately, but go nuts and add all the goodness you like with one of the extra ingredients. I love this with a little dash of coconut milk and maple syrup! Delicious.

Dirty beans on toast is a twist on an old favourite. It is a breakfast packed with fibre and protein, but the chillies make it the perfect hangover cure. Whether you had a late night or you just want to kick off your day with a bang, dirty beans on toast is a winner.

## Dirty beans on toast

SERVES 2

Olive oil, for frying

3 garlic cloves, finely chopped

3 jalapeños, roughly chopped

2 green chillies, deseeded and finely chopped

1 tsp smoked paprika

1 x 400g tin haricot beans, rinsed and drained

1 x 400g tin pinto beans, rinsed and drained

2 tbsp BBQ sauce

250ml (1 cup) passata

¼ loaf of your favourite unsliced bread

Chopped coriander, to garnish

Onion salt and garlic pepper, to taste (optional)

Drizzle the olive oil into a pan over a low heat. Add the garlic, jalapeños and chillies and fry for a few minutes.

Add the smoked paprika, stirring to coat the garlic and chillies, then add all the beans, BBQ sauce and passata and mix together. Simmer over a low heat for 15 minutes to allow the sauce to thicken, stirring occasionally.

While the beans simmer, add a generous drizzle of olive oil to a frying pan set over a medium heat. Once the oil has begun to smoke slightly, cut two thick slices of bread and place them in the pan. Fry for just over a minute until lightly browned and crispy, then turn over and cook on the other side.

Place a slice of bread on each plate and cover each with the bean mixture. Sprinkle over the coriander, onion salt and garlic pepper, if using, and serve with a smile!

This is a really delicious breakfast that feels like a dessert! Because of the low sugar, healthy fats and high protein content, there is no reason you shouldn't go ahead and treat yourself in the morning!

# Chocolate orange chia pudding

SERVES 2

6 tbsp chia seeds

500ml (2 cups) cashew milk plus 2 tbsp

1 avocado, halved, peeled and stoned

1 tbsp maple syrup (optional)

2 tbsp cocoa powder

2 seedless oranges, divided into segments

Grated vegan dark chocolate or cocoa nibs, to decorate (optional)

Divide the chia seeds among two glasses or jars, then pour a quarter of the milk into each and stir with a fork. Jars are perfect for this because you can seal them with a lid, so if you are using a glass, cover it so it is airtight. Leave in the fridge to set for at least 3 hours.

Once the seeds have soaked up all the liquid, blend the avocado with the remaining 2 tablespoons cashew milk, the maple syrup, if using, and cocoa powder in a blender until smooth.

Add half the orange segments to each serving of the chia seed mixture, followed by the avocado and chocolate mixture, then top with the remaining orange segments. You can sprinkle some grated dark chocolate or cocoa nibs over, if you like!

TIP
You can make a large batch of the chia pudding by scaling up the quantities. It will keep in an airtight container in the fridge for a week.

Vegan French toast is amazing! Add apple and cinnamon and you have a party on your hands. This is the perfect breakfast to really show off with. Make this for someone special as a breakfast in bed and you have a permanent place in their good books.

# Apple and cinnamon French toast

SERVES 2

1 tbsp chia seeds
2 tbsp flaxseeds
½ tsp ground cinnamon
2 tbsp apple sauce (or just blend some apple in a blender, or cook chopped apple until pulpy)
60ml (¼ cup) maple syrup, plus extra to serve
250ml (1 cup) cashew milk or oat milk
1 tsp vanilla extract
2 slices of sourdough bread
Oil, for frying
Fruit, to serve
Icing sugar, for dusting (optional)

Put the chia seeds, flaxseeds and cinnamon into a blender and pulse until finely ground. Add the apple sauce, maple syrup, milk and vanilla and blend until smooth.

Pour the mixture into a wide bowl, then add the bread, one slice at a time, pressing down on it to make sure the mixture soaks right into it.

Add a little oil to a frying pan set over a medium heat, then when hot, add the bread slices one at a time if necessary, and cook for a couple of minutes on each side until golden brown.

Serve hot, with some fresh fruit and a drizzle of maple syrup or a little dusting of icing sugar.

Vegan and omelette might not be two words you ever thought you'd see combined, but I am here to tell you that you're missing out if you've not yet tried this delicious dish. Slightly firmer than a traditional omelette, this vegan version has tons more flavour and there's no harm done.

# Vegan omelette

SERVES 2

175g silken tofu

2 tbsp (½ cup) nutritional yeast

60g (¼ cup) gram (chickpea) flour

1½ tsp cornflour or arrowroot

¼ tsp ground turmeric

Large pinch of smoked paprika

½ tsp salt

125ml (½ cup) aquafaba (juice from a tin of chickpeas)

1 tbsp olive oil, plus extra for frying

Salt and black pepper, to taste

*Suggested fillings (optional)*

Vegan cheese

Wilted spinach

Chopped tomatoes

Dijon mustard

Add all the omelette ingredients to a blender and blitz until the mixture is smooth and there are no lumps. If it looks too thick to pour, add a splash more aquafaba. If you want to add vegan cheese to your omelette, stir it in now.

Heat a little olive oil in a large frying pan over a medium heat. When the pan and the oil are hot, pour in half of the batter mixture and tilt the pan to coat the base with the batter.

At this stage, add any of the fillings – I suggest chopped spinach and tomatoes, but go crazy and make it how you would a regular omelette. Cook for just over a minute, then carefully flip the omelette using a spatula and cook on the other side until browned.

Serve hot with a pinch of salt and pepper to taste. Repeat with the other half of the mixture to make your second omelette.

TIP
This omelette is also great eaten cold – you can cut it up and make it into egg sarnies with a little vegan mayo and some spring onions scattered over.

Eggs Benedict is a long-standing breakfast classic served in hotels, restaurants and cafés all across the world. Here's my vegan twist, made with seasoned tofu and a delicious vegan hollandaise. You can use the hollandaise recipes for dipping asparagus too!

# Benedict of the doubt

SERVES 2

½ tsp smoked paprika

1 tsp dried oregano

1 tsp garlic pepper

½ tsp onion salt

175g firm tofu

Oil, for brushing and frying

2 shallots or 1 small white onion, finely chopped

2 large tomatoes, cut in half

50g fresh spinach

2 muffins (check the label for eggs and milk, wholemeal usually don't contain any)

*For the vegan hollandaise*

60g (½ cup) cashews

Juice of ½ lemon

½ tsp salt

½ tsp garlic powder

⅓ tsp ground turmeric

1 tsp Dijon mustard

Start by making the hollandaise sauce. Soak the cashews for 1–2 hours in 125ml (½ cup) water and the lemon juice – this helps to break down the phytic acid in the nuts, making them easier to digest.

Drain and rinse the cashews under cold water in a sieve, then add to a blender with the remaining ingredients and blend to smooth consistency. Set aside.

Using a pestle and mortar, grind all the seasonings – paprika, oregano, garlic pepper and onion salt – to a fine powder, then tip out on to a flat plate.

Cut the tofu in half and dab with kitchen paper to remove any moisture. Brush the tofu slices with oil and press them into the seasoning to coat on all sides.

Heat a little oil in a pan over a medium heat, then add the shallots, tomato halves and tofu and fry for 10 minutes, turning the tofu every couple of minutes to brown on all sides.

Wilt the spinach in a separate pan with a little water over a low heat, then scoop out with a slotted spoon and stir into the tofu. Cook for 1 minute.

Meanwhile, halve the muffins and toast lightly. Warm the hollandaise sauce in a pan over a low heat.

Put the muffin halves on two plates and layer the spinach, tofu and tomato on top, then a dollop of warm hollandaise sauce. Garnish with a dusting of smoked paprika and serve immediately.

# ON THE GO

## QUICK BITES

Vegan pesto

Pesto muffins

Pesto stuffed mushrooms

Pesto avocado toast

Classic bruschetta

Epic bruschetta

Carrot and coriander soup

Wholesome tomato soup

Garlic mushrooms

Peppered cashew cheese sauce

PB&J toastie

---

## PERFECT FOR PACKED LUNCHES

Smoky bean stew

Raw pad thai

Peanut butter and tofu sarnie

Tomato tapenade

Sweet and smoky sandwich

Spicy bean sandwich

Mushroom and pesto sandwich

Grilled aubergine sub sandwich

Watermelon salad

Courgetti and pesto

Smoky butternut farro risotto

Pesto is my favourite sauce! I love it on everything. I could create
a book dedicated to it (and I might), so this is my pesto recipe that
you can use time after time and pair with all kinds of delicious dishes.
Add vegan cheese for extra decadence and an added melty bonus.

# Vegan pesto

MAKES 1 JAR

70g (½ cup) pine nuts

3 large garlic cloves,
    roughly chopped

¼ tsp sea salt, plus more
    to taste

½ tsp black pepper

1 tbsp (¼ cup) nutritional
    yeast

50g (2 cups) roughly
    chopped basil leaves

50g strong vegan cheese,
    grated (optional)

Juice of ½ lemon

4 tbsp extra virgin olive oil

Bash the pine nuts using a large pestle and mortar
to break them up, then grind to a dense paste.

Add the garlic, salt, pepper and nutritional yeast
and grind into the nut paste.

Add the basil leaves (fine stems are ok but avoid
large stalks) and begin to bash the leaves down until
they become darker and moist, then blend them into
the paste. Scatter in the vegan cheese now, if using,
blending it into the pesto evenly.

Lastly, pour the lemon and oil into the pesto mix
slowly, a little at a time, stirring it to your preferred
consistency.

If you are looking for a quick alternative method,
just add the ingredients to a blender and blend
until smooth.

Store in a jar and use within a week.

Pesto muffins are perfect for snacking on the go. Try them with my Wholesome tomato soup (see page 49).

# Pesto muffins

MAKES 12

250g (2 cups) plain flour
2½ tsp baking powder
½ tsp salt
310ml (1¼ cups) oat milk
60ml (¼ cup) olive oil
1 tbsp ground flaxseed
1½ large courgettes
60ml (¼ cup) Vegan pesto
　(see page 40)
Basil leaves, to serve

Preheat the oven to 200°C/180°C Fan/400°F/gas 6 and grease the cups of a 12-hole muffin tin.

In a large bowl, mix together the flour, baking powder and salt.

In a small bowl, combine the milk, olive oil and ground flaxseed. Let the flax sit for 5 minutes. Grate the courgettes, setting aside a few tablespoons for decoration after baking.

Add all the wet ingredients to the dry ingredients and stir until combined. Tip in the grated courgette and pesto and stir to combine all the ingredients, until a batter is formed. Spoon the batter among the greased muffin holes and place the tin in the oven. Bake for 20 minutes, or until golden brown on top and cooked through. Allow to cool before serving.

Top with courgette shavings and basil leaves, and serve.

Stuffed mushrooms are so versatile. Serve them with chips, sliced for a creamy pasta dish or surrounded by roasted veggies. Such a useful and tasty recipe.

## Pesto stuffed mushrooms

SERVES 2

4 portobello mushrooms
Olive oil, for brushing
4 tbsp Vegan pesto (see
    page 40)

Wipe the mushrooms with damp kitchen paper to remove any dirt, then brush all over with olive oil. Turn the mushrooms upside down, remove the stalks and pack 1 tablespoon of pesto into each mushroom.

Place under a medium grill for 10 minutes until browning. Serve immediately.

Avocado toast has become a vegan staple. But, done right it is a thing of beauty. Give this recipe a try – you'll ask yourself why you ever did it another way!

## Pesto avocado toast

SERVES 1

2 slices of sourdough
   bread
2 tbsp olive oil
2 tbsp Vegan pesto (see
   page 40)
1 large avocado
Basil leaves (optional)
Pine nuts (optional)

Brush the sourdough slices with the olive oil on one side. Heat a ridged frying pan and griddle the sourdough until crispy and golden brown. Remove the bread from the pan and spread the pesto over the crispy side.

Cut the avocado in half, remove the stone, then peel away the skin. Slice the avocado very thinly. With one half, slide your blade underneath the avocado and gently splay the avocado into a fan before sliding it onto the bread. With the second half you can either repeat that process or make an avocado rose – take the thinly sliced avocado and fan it out so that each slice half-covers the slices on either side of it. Then, starting at one end, roll the avocado into a spiral (if in doubt, see the Epivegan YouTube channel for more instructions). Slide a knife under the rose and place on the bread, then fan it out.

Sprinkle with pine nuts and basil leaves, if you like, and serve.

Classic bruschetta is a must; it's a traditional Italian dish that is so simple it's perfect. It makes an ideal canapé or starter, or is great for an alfresco summer picnic.

## Classic bruschetta

SERVES 2

4 slices of sourdough
    bread (cut into 1cm/½in
    slices)
3 garlic cloves, 1 cut in half,
    2 thinly sliced
Olive oil, for frying and
    drizzling
8 cherry tomatoes, sliced
Small bunch of basil,
    leaves roughly chopped

Rub each slice of sourdough bread with the cut halves of garlic.

Heat a little olive oil in a frying pan and fry the bread for just over a minute on each side until crunchy and golden brown – you may need to do this in batches.

Top the toasted sourdough with the garlic slices and tomatoes. Scatter over the chopped basil leaves, drizzle with olive oil and serve immediately.

The brilliant thing about bruschetta is that you can customise it any way you like to include your favourite ingredients. This is my preferred way to make it.

# Epic bruschetta

SERVES 2

4 slices of sourdough
  bread (cut into 1cm/½in
  slices)
3 garlic cloves, 1 cut in half,
  2 thinly sliced
Olive oil, for frying and
  drizzling
8 thin asparagus stems,
  woody ends removed
8 cherry tomatoes, sliced
2 ripe figs, sliced (or use
  grapes for the same
  sweetness)
Rocket leaves

Rub each slice of sourdough bread with the cut halves of garlic.

Heat a little olive oil in a frying pan and fry the asparagus for 10 minutes until lightly coloured and cooked through with a little bite. Remove from the pan and set aside.

Toast the bread in the same pan for just over a minute on each side until crunchy and golden brown – you may need to do this in batches.

Top the toasted sourdough with the garlic slices and tomatoes. Add a few slices of the figs or grapes, then add a few asparagus stems and top with a handful of rocket. Drizzle with olive oil and serve immediately.

An autumn or winter warmer that's perfect served with a crusty roll or toastie. A classic, easy and tasty soup.

# Carrot and coriander soup

SERVES 4

Oil, for frying
½ white onion, diced
3 garlic cloves, chopped
½ tsp ground cumin
Pinch of salt and black
  pepper
4 large carrots, peeled and
  roughly chopped
1 medium white potato,
  peeled and roughly
  chopped
Large bunch of coriander

Heat the oil in a pan, then fry the onion and garlic for a couple of minutes over a low heat until softened.

Add the cumin, salt and pepper, then pour in 1 litre (4 cups) water and bring to the boil over a high heat.

Once boiling, add the carrots and potatoes and cook for 15 minutes until the potatoes are tender.

Remove from the heat, scoop out the vegetables using a slotted spoon and transfer to a blender. Add two ladles of the cooking liquid and most of the coriander and blend to a smooth consistency.

Return to the pan and heat through, then serve garnished with the reserved coriander leaves.

Tomato soup is often undersold, associated with something out of a tin. But this tomato soup is a wholesome, delicious dish that will rekindle your love for a classic.

# Wholesome tomato soup

SERVES 6

3 tbsp extra virgin olive oil, plus extra for drizzling

1 large carrot, finely chopped

3 long shallots, finely chopped

4 garlic cloves, finely chopped

1 red chilli, finely chopped

500g tomatoes on the vine

300ml passata, sieved

2 tsp salt

2 tsp cracked black pepper

3 tsp Vegan pesto (see page 40)

25g basil leaves

Heat the extra virgin olive oil in a large pan set over a low heat. Add the carrot, shallots, garlic and chilli and gently fry for 5 minutes.

Snip the vine tomatoes from the main stem but leave their individual stems attached, then pierce each one with a sharp knife and add to the pan, whole, for a further 10 minutes.

Pour in 250ml (1 cup) water and the passata, season with the salt and pepper, stir, then leave to simmer for 10 minutes.

Transfer everything to a blender and blend to a smooth soup.

Before serving, return the soup to the pan and heat gently over a low heat, stirring in the pesto and basil leaves just before removing from the heat.

Serve with a drizzle of olive oil and a toastie or some crusty bread.

Garlic and mushrooms are a perfect combination and so versatile. They are great as a topping for a jacket potato, on the side of a curry or on toast – or how about adding soy cream and serving them with tagliatelle? However you eat them, you can't go wrong.

# Garlic mushrooms

SERVES 4 AS A SIDE

5 tbsp olive oil

4 garlic cloves, very finely chopped

375g white mushrooms, cut into quarters

¼ tsp salt, or to taste

2 tsp chopped parsley

Small bunch of wild garlic, chopped (optional)

Heat the oil in a large frying pan over a medium heat. Add the garlic and cook, stirring.

Add the mushrooms to the pan and cook, stirring, for 10–12 minutes until tender.

Remove from the heat, sprinkle with the parsley and wild garlic, if using, and serve nice and hot.

TIP
These garlic mushrooms are great in the Spanish frittata on page 161 – just replace the potatoes and peppers with these garlic mushrooms to really mix things up!

Raw cashew cheese sauce is a real favourite of mine. The first time I made this was while interviewing my friend, the freerunner, Ninja Warrior and spiritual guru, Tim Shieff. The peppercorns add a little heat here, which perks up the other dishes I pair this with, but if you prefer you can remove them for a subtler taste.

## Peppered cashew cheese sauce

SERVES 4 AS A SIDE

125g (1 cup) cashews
2 tsp black peppercorns
1 yellow pepper, deseeded
    and roughly chopped
2 tbsp (½ cup) nutritional
    yeast
1 tbsp lemon juice
2 garlic cloves
1 tsp apple cider vinegar
Pinch of sea salt (smoked
    is best)
½ tsp smoked paprika

Soak the cashews in a small bowl of water for 1 hour, then drain and rinse under cold running water in a sieve. Set aside.

Put the peppercorns into a blender and pulse to break them up. Tip in the cashews and whizz again to blend, then add in all the other ingredients and blend to a smooth cheese sauce.

TIP
Use this tasty sauce in: Spicy bean sandwich (see page 61), Sweet potato salad (see page 87) and Hash daddy (see page 148).

Peanut butter and jelly/jam toastie is a traditional American sandwich in a golden-brown, crunchy package. Delicious as lunch, a snack or with ice cream as a dessert. Doesn't it just sell itself?

# PB&J toastie

SERVES 1

Vegan butter, for spreading
and for frying
2 slices of bread
1 tbsp peanut butter
2 tsp jam (jelly)

Spread some butter on a slice of bread, add a layer of peanut butter then a dollop of jam. Spread the filling over the bread slice, leaving ½cm (¼in) clear at the edge of the crust.

Sandwich the other slice of bread on top and press firmly around the outside to seal the filling inside.

Add a tablespoon of butter to a frying pan set over a very low heat. When the butter has melted and is starting to smoke slightly, add the toastie and fry on both sides until golden brown. Serve hot.

This dish is not only bright and tasty to look at, but it really delivers on flavour. I created this recipe one day when my parents didn't know what to eat for lunch – it left them very happy and satisfied.

# Smoky bean stew

SERVES 4

Olive oil, for frying
3 shallots, finely chopped
1 jalapeño chilli, finely
    chopped
2 garlic cloves, finely
    chopped
1 x 400g tin aduki beans
    (or you can use black
    beans or haricot), rinsed
    and drained
1 x 198g tin sweetcorn,
    drained
1 tsp chilli paste
½ tsp smoked paprika
1 tbsp garlic purée
Pinch of black pepper
300g passata
Juice of ½ lemon or lime

*To serve*
1 avocado
4 tbsp plant-based yoghurt
2 handfuls of spinach
    leaves
Small bunch of coriander

Heat some olive oil in a pan, then add the shallots, chilli and garlic and cook over a medium heat until softened.

Tip in all the remaining ingredients, along with 125ml (½ cup) water. Stir to combine, then simmer for 20 minutes to thicken, stirring occasionally.

Serve hot with any toppings of your choice.

I first cooked this for commentator John Gooden during an interview; it's bright, tasty and full of goodness. It is fantastic if you are looking to eat more healthy raw food without feeling like you are missing out on anything.

# Raw pad thai

SERVES 4

5 spring onions, finely chopped

1 red pepper, deseeded and finely chopped

⅓ red or white cabbage, finely chopped

1 red and 1 green chilli, finely chopped

100g sugar snap peas, roughly chopped

1 pak choi, roughly chopped

Handful of Thai basil, roughly chopped

2 courgettes, spiralized

2 sweet potatoes, spiralized

1 large carrot, spiralized

Juice of 1 lime

Handful of crushed nuts

1 tbsp sesame seeds

1 tbsp pumpkin seeds

1 tsp flaxseeds

*For the satay sauce*

3 tbsp raw peanut butter

1 tbsp garlic purée

3 tbsp maple syrup

2 tbsp cold-pressed hemp oil or coconut oil

Combine the chopped spring onions, pepper, cabbage and chillies with the sugar snap peas, pak choi and Thai basil in a large serving bowl.

To make the satay sauce, in a small bowl, mix together the peanut butter, garlic purée, maple syrup and oil to make a smooth sauce.

Drizzle the satay sauce over the spiralized vegetables, and toss to coat. Squeeze over the lime juice, scatter over the nuts and seeds and the chopped veg and serve immediately.

TIP
If you don't have a spiralizer, use a peeler and slice the strips into noodles.

Don't judge a book by its cover! This tasty sandwich is a great addition to your packed lunch arsenal, stuffed with crispy fried cabbage, sweet peanut butter and tofu goodness.

# Peanut butter and tofu sarnie

SERVES 1

Perfect for packed lunches

Drizzle of oil

25g thinly sliced white cabbage

1 tsp garlic purée

1 red chilli, deseeded and thinly sliced

100g firm tofu, cut into 3 slices

1 tsp soy sauce

Sprinkle of sesame seeds

1 spring onion, thinly sliced

1 tsp peanut butter

2 thick slices of bread

Heat some oil in a large frying pan, and when hot add the sliced cabbage with the garlic purée and chilli. Stir to combine and fry for 5 minutes.

Add the tofu slices to the pan with the soy sauce and fry lightly on both sides. Sprinkle half the sesame seeds into the pan and take off the heat.

Spread a thick layer of peanut butter over both slices of bread, then top one with the tofu and cabbage mix. Scatter over the thinly sliced spring onion and the remaining sesame seeds, then top with the second slice of bread. Cut into quarters and serve.

Great in a sandwich, as a dip for dough balls or stirred through pasta. Tomato tapenade is fantastic for when you want some rich, intense flavour in your life.

# Tomato tapenade

MAKES 1 JAR

500g small tomatoes, cut into quarters

3 garlic cloves, very finely chopped

2 tbsp extra virgin olive oil

75g (½ cup) Kalamata olives, pitted and chopped

1 tbsp balsamic vinegar

1 tsp smoked salt

½ tsp freshly ground black pepper

¼ tsp smoked paprika flakes

1 tsp rosemary, finely chopped

1 tsp fresh thyme, finely chopped

1 tsp brown sugar

Preheat the oven to 150°C/130°C Fan/300°F/gas 2.

Put the tomatoes into a bowl with the garlic, oil, olives and balsamic vinegar and mix everything together to coat. Tip out on to a baking tray and season with the salt, pepper, paprika flakes, rosemary, thyme and sugar and roast for 35 minutes.

Allow the ingredients to cool then add to a blender and pulse to blend – you don't want the consistency too fine, just slightly lumpier than a pesto.

Serve as a dip or spread.

You can store this in a jar and use within a week.

Sweet, smoky goodness in a crusty bread package. This sandwich has a whole lot going on but everything works so well together. See photo on pages 62–63.

# Sweet and smoky sandwich

SERVES 1

Small baguette, about 20cm (4in) long
1 tbsp Tomato tapenade (see page 59)
1 tsp Vegan pesto (see page 40)
½ cooked sweet potato
2 cherry tomatoes, thinly sliced
1 spring onion, roughly chopped
Broccoli sprouts or cress (optional)
Small handful of rocket

Cut the bread three-quarters of the way through horizontally and carefully open it out so it doesn't tear apart completely. Spread the tapenade on the bottom half and the pesto on the lid half of the loaf.

Spread the sweet potato over the tapenade and mash slightly with a fork. Top with the sliced cherry tomatoes and sprinkle over the spring onion, broccoli sprouts or cress, if using, and rocket.

Close, press together to seal everything in and enjoy!

This is based on the best sandwich I ever ate. I was travelling through Scandinavia in winter and wandered into a beautiful café to get out of the cold. This warmed me right up and put a smile on my face, so I've made my own version for you to try! Try it with a teaspoon of Peppered cashew cheese sauce (see page 52). See photo on pages 62–63.

# Spicy bean sandwich

SERVES 1

1 red pepper, cut in half and deseeded

1 x 400g tin kidney beans, rinsed and drained

¼ tsp chilli flakes

¼ tsp salt

1 tsp oil

Small baguette, about 20cm (4in) long

Vegan mayo, for spreading (optional)

10g thinly sliced white cabbage

Vegan cheese (optional)

2 cherry tomatoes, thinly sliced

2 jalapeño chillies, thinly sliced

½ thinly sliced avocado

Handful of rocket

Turn the grill to a low heat.

Place the red pepper halves flat on the grill pan and cook for 5 minutes, or until soft and slightly blackened, then turn over and cook on the other side. Remove from the heat and when cool, slice thinly.

Tip the kidneys beans into a small bowl. Add the chilli flakes, salt and oil and mash to a smooth paste.

If you're eating immediately, slice the bread in half. If it's a packed lunch, cut the bread three-quarters of the way through horizontally and carefully open it out so it doesn't tear apart completely. Spread the bean spread on the bottom half and the mayo on the top half, if using. Top the kidney bean spread with the thinly sliced white cabbage and the grilled pepper, followed by vegan cheese if you are using it. Lastly, add the tomatoes, jalapeños and sprinkle with rocket leaves. Close up and enjoy!

Portobello mushroom's little cousin the Portobellini is mouth-watering when brushed with pesto and grilled. It's what makes this sandwich such a winner. Eat it warm, take it for lunch or on a picnic. Wherever you eat it, it's a taste sensation. See photo on pages 62–63.

# Mushroom and pesto sandwich

SERVES 1

2 tbsp olive oil

2 tsp Vegan pesto (see page 40)

1 tbsp finely chopped garlic or garlic purée

1–2 Portobellini mushrooms

Small baguette, about 20cm (4in) long

1 tomato, thinly sliced

Handful of peppery salad leaves

Cracked black pepper, to taste

Heat the grill to a low heat.

Combine the oil, pesto and garlic in a small bowl then brush or drizzle this mix over the mushrooms.

Place the mushrooms on a grill pan and grill for 10 minutes.

If you're eating immediately, slice the bread in half. If it's a packed lunch, cut the bread three-quarters of the way through horizontally and carefully open it out so it doesn't tear apart completely. Layer the tomato slices on the bottom half of the loaf, followed by the mushroom, then top with the salad and season with pepper to taste. Close up and eat!

Grilled aubergine seasoned with Mediterranean herbs is an Italian classic. Construct an aubergine marinara sub and it's pure comfort food. Satisfaction guaranteed. See photo on pages 62–63.

# Grilled aubergine sub sandwich

SERVES 1

Olive oil, for brushing
1 garlic clove, very finely chopped
2 slices of aubergine, cut thinly lengthways
Dried oregano, to taste
Salt and pepper, to taste
Small baguette, about 20cm (4in) long
1 tsp Vegan pesto (see page 40)
1 tbsp Marinara sauce (see page 75)
Handful of rocket leaves
1 large Brazil nut

Heat the grill to a medium heat.

Combine the olive oil and garlic in a little bowl, then brush this over the aubergine slices and season with oregano, salt and pepper, then grill for 5–10 minutes.

If you're eating immediately, slice the bread in half. If it's a packed lunch, cut the bread three-quarters of the way through horizontally and carefully open it out so it doesn't tear apart completely. Spread the pesto on the bottom half of the loaf, then layer over the grilled aubergine slices and drizzle over the marinara sauce. Top with rocket and grate over the Brazil nut.

Press the two halves together and enjoy warm or cold.

This is an incredibly fresh, hydrating, raw salad that's perfect for a hot summer's day. For cooler days, the subtle heat coming from the chilli will warm you up. In my book, whatever it is, add watermelon and it just gets better!

# Watermelon salad

SERVES 2

2 baby gem lettuce leaves
1 celery stick, thinly sliced
300g (2 cups) watermelon
  cubes
100g (1 cup) green seedless
  grapes, cut in half
1 green chilli, thinly sliced
1 avocado, halved, stoned
  and thinly sliced
Handful of mint leaves,
  torn
Juice of ½ lime
Salt, to taste

Roughly tear the baby gem leaves and put them in a serving bowl. Add the celery, watermelon cubes, grape halves and chilli and toss everything together.

Drape the avocado slices on top, scatter over the torn mint and drizzle over the lime juice. Season with a pinch of salt and serve.

This classic raw dish is a real go-to for me. I have added my own touches here for a little something extra. For the very best flavour, remove the ingredients from the fridge at least an hour before preparing this and let them come up to room temperature.

## Courgetti and pesto

SERVES 2

1 ripe avocado, cut in half and stoned

3 tbsp Vegan pesto (see page 40)

Juice of ½ lemon

2 courgettes, spiralized (or use a peeler if you don't have a spiralizer)

Handful of cherry tomatoes, cut in half

2 tbsp (½ cup) nutritional yeast

5 Brazil nuts, grated

Scoop out the avocado flesh and mash it in a bowl with the pesto and a squeeze of lemon juice.

Stir through the spiralized courgette to coat with the pesto mix, then stir in the chopped cherry tomatoes.

Top with the nutritional yeast and grated Brazil nuts and enjoy.

Farro wheat is a tasty wholesome grain that fills you up and leaves you satisfied. So here I've switched out the rice and created this farro risotto to mix things up.

# Smoky butternut farro risotto

SERVES 2

250g (3 cups) quick-cook farro wheat

55g (½ cup) frozen peas

200g (1 cup) frozen butternut squash chunks

1 onion, thinly sliced

3 garlic cloves, thinly sliced

1 tbsp olive oil

1 tsp dried thyme

250ml (1 cup) soy cream

1 tsp onion salt

1 tsp smoked paprika

12 asparagus or Tenderstem broccoli stems

Bring a pan of water to the boil and add the farro, peas and butternut squash chunks, then cook over a medium heat for 10 minutes.

Meanwhile, add the onion and garlic to a pan with the olive oil and thyme and fry over a low heat for 3 minutes. Then stir in the soy cream, onion salt and smoked paprika.

Thoroughly drain the butternut squash, peas and farro and tip into the cream sauce. Stir to combine and break up the butternut squash a little, then cook over a low heat for 10 minutes to thicken.

Meanwhile, cook the asparagus or broccoli on a hot griddle to soften it slightly but still retain some crunch.

Serve the smoky butternut farro covered with three stems of asparagus or broccoli per person. Enjoy!

# FOR MAINS

## LUNCH EVERY DAY

Arancini

Arrabbiata sauce

Marinara sauce

Green pea and pesto soup

French onion soup

Bean minestrone

Chickpea tuna baked potato

Broccoli bowl

Asparagus salad

Warm Italian salad

Green pea bowl

Sweet potato salad

## DINNER EVERY DAY

Mushroom tagliatelle

Cottage pie

Protein-packed peppers

Cauliflower steaks

Pasta e fagioli

Linguini fusion

Sausage and lentil casserole

Sag aloo

Savoury 'biscuits' with mushroom gravy

Roasted new potatoes with garlic aioli

One of my all-time favourite meals is the crunchy, tasty, classic arancini. These risotto balls are perfect for using up leftover risotto, although, if you are like me, once you've tried these you will be making too much risotto every time, with these little arancini bites in mind. These are best served with Arrabbiata sauce (see page 74).

# Arancini

SERVES 4 AS A SIDE

1 tbsp Vegan pesto (see page 40)
800g (4 cups) leftover risotto
2 tbsp plain flour
2 tbsp oat milk
2 tsp dried thyme
1 tbsp ground flaxseed
75g panko breadcrumbs
Salt and pepper, to taste
Olive oil, for frying

Mix the pesto into the risotto and divide it up evenly – the balls you make should each be about half the size of a golf ball at most, this is so the inside cooks through without the outside burning.

Put the flour on to a plate and roll the balls in the flour – they only need a very thin coating.

Pour the oat milk into another bowl and roll the flour-dusted balls in it; again, they only need a thin coating.

In a deep dish, mix together the thyme, flaxseed and panko breadcrumbs with some salt and pepper. Roll the balls in this, making sure each is completely covered.

Once all the balls are coated, heat some oil in a frying pan and lightly fry all of the balls over a medium heat until they are golden brown. Serve with your favourite sauce.

Arrabbiata sauce is the spicy tomato sauce for any scenario. It's great paired with Arancini (see photo on previous page), but it's also perfect with pasta.

## Arrabbiata sauce

SERVES 4 AS A DIP

Olive oil, for cooking
3 garlic cloves, thinly sliced
1 red chilli, thinly sliced
Handful of basil, stalks and
   leaves finely chopped
   (or use 3 tsp dried), plus
   extra leaves to garnish
250ml (1 cup) passata

Heat some olive oil in a pan over a low heat, then fry the garlic and chilli for 1 minute. Add the chopped basil and then the passata and simmer for 10 minutes until thickened.

Serve with a few basil leaves.

A classic that you must have in your back pocket! Perfect on pasta, great for lasagne, ideal for pizza – it's an all-rounder for those nights when you just don't know what to eat. If you have all of these ingredients to hand, then you have some seriously tasty options. Get the best quality tinned tomatoes you can, it makes all the difference.

## Marinara sauce

SERVES 4

Drizzle of olive oil
1 small onion, finely
    chopped
3 garlic cloves, finely
    chopped
½ tsp salt
Pinch of black pepper
1 tsp dried oregano
½ tsp sugar
400g tinned plum
    tomatoes
25g basil leaves, roughly
    chopped (optional)

Add a generous drizzle of olive oil to a large pan and set over a low heat. Add the onion and garlic and fry over a very low heat for 5 minutes. Add the salt, pepper, oregano and sugar and stir.

Tip in the tomatoes and use a wooden spoon or spatula to stir and break them up. Simmer over a low heat for 30 minutes to thicken the sauce.

If you like, stir through the roughly chopped basil just before serving.

Looking for a fresh, warming soup that is packed full of flavour?
Look no further! Green pea and pesto soup is a comforting classic.

# Green pea and pesto soup

SERVES 2

220g (2 cups) frozen peas

3 garlic cloves, finely
  chopped

1 tbsp olive oil

30g (1 cup) spinach leaves

4 tsp Vegan pesto (see
  page 40)

Pinch of garlic pepper
  (optional)

Pinch of onion salt

Boil 250ml (1 cup) water in a pan, then take off the heat and add half the frozen peas. Leave to cook in the heat for 5 minutes. Tip the water and peas into a blender and blitz to a smooth paste.

Meanwhile, add the garlic to the same pan with the olive oil and fry over a low heat for 3 minutes. Add the remaining frozen peas and the spinach. Now add the blended pea mixture and stir.

Stir in the pesto and, if you are using it, the garlic pepper and onion salt. Give everything a stir before leaving to simmer over a low heat for 10 minutes.

Serve hot with some warm fresh bread.

Traditional French onion soup is such a classic, but it's not complete without a rich cheesy crouton, so I've included a vegan version for you here. For really cheesy croutons, use an intensely flavoured cheddar-style grated cheese like one from Sainsbury's Freefrom range, or Follow Your Heart pizza shreds or Sheese also melt well – these are available in larger supermarkets or in health food stores.

# French onion soup

SERVES 4

Olive oil, for frying

4 garlic cloves, finely chopped

3 large onions, sliced paper thin

3 shallots, thinly sliced

1 tbsp sugar

Pinch of onion salt

1 tbsp plain flour

Drizzle of white wine

1 garlic stock cube

1 vegetable stock cube

*For the croutons*

4 slices of bread, crusts removed

Olive oil, for brushing

80g vegan cheese (optional)

2 tbsp (½ cup) nutritional yeast (optional)

Heat the oil in a large pan and add the garlic, onions and shallots. Stir in the sugar and gently cook for 10 minutes over a low heat. Add the onion salt, flour and the white wine to the pan.

Boil 250ml (1 cup) water in a kettle, then pour over the garlic and vegetable stock cubes in a heatproof jug. Stir to dissolve, then pour into the onion mixture and simmer over a medium heat for 10 minutes.

While the soup is simmering, preheat the oven to 160°C/140°C Fan/325°F/gas 3. Brush the slices of bread with olive oil on both sides. Place on a baking tray and bake in the oven for 10 minutes on each side until golden brown and crunchy.

When the soup is ready to serve, ladle it into small ovenproof bowls and top with the croutons. Cover the toasts with vegan cheese, if using, and heat in the oven until the cheese has completely melted. If you are not using vegan cheese then skip the oven step, and instead top with the crouton and sprinkle each with some nutritional yeast before serving.

Minestrone is comfort food at its finest. Beans and pasta in a warming broth makes a healthy, tasty bowl of goodness. It is also a great recipe for making in bulk and freezing for another day.

# Bean minestrone

SERVES 4

1 large onion, diced
2 tbsp olive oil
3 rocket chillies, finely chopped
Pinch of onion salt
1 tsp chilli purée
1 tbsp tomato purée
1 x 400g tin green lentils
1 x 400g tin cannellini beans
½ x 400g tin butter beans
½ x 400g tin red kidney beans
100g (1 cup) macaroni
1 garlic stock cube
Chopped parsley, to garnish

Cook the onion in a large pan with the olive oil over a low heat. Add the chillies to the pan and cook for 5 minutes. Add the onion salt, chilli purée, tomato purée, the lentils and beans and their liquids and cook over a medium heat for 5 minutes. Pour in 300ml (1¼ cups) boiling water and the macaroni and stir. Crumble in the garlic stock cube, put the lid on the pan and simmer for 15 minutes. Then remove the lid and allow to thicken for 5 minutes, stirring occasionally.

Remove the pan from the heat and leave to cool for 2–3 minutes. Serve garnished with chopped parsley. Enjoy.

Chickpea 'tuna' is a vegan classic, and when paired with baked potato you have a go-to meal that is always there when you need it. It's great as a packed lunch, too – pack the chickpea tuna in a separate box and add to a baked potato at work or you can eat it on the go.

# Chickpea tuna baked potato

SERVES 2

2 large baking potatoes

Olive oil, for baking

1 x 400g tin chickpeas, rinsed and drained

50g spring onions, chopped

½ red onion, finely diced

125g (¼ cup) vegan hummus (check the label – some contain milk)

Juice of ½ lemon

½ tsp garlic powder or finely chopped garlic

2 tbsp chopped dill (optional)

½ x 198g tin sweetcorn, drained

1 tsp vegan mayo (optional)

Salt and pepper, to taste

*To serve*

Vegan butter

50g vegan cheese (optional)

Preheat the oven to 220°C/200°C Fan/425°F/gas 7.

Wash and dry the potatoes and pierce them 2–3 times with a fork. Rub them all over with oil then wrap in tin foil, place on a baking sheet and bake in the oven for 50 minutes.

While the potatoes are baking, tip the chickpeas into a bowl and use the back of a fork or a masher to mash them to the desired consistency. I like it slightly chunky. Add the remaining ingredients and mix well, then season with salt and pepper to taste.

Remove the potatoes from the oven (if you like them crispy, remove the foil and bake for a further 10 minutes). Cut a cross into the top of the potatoes and squeeze the sides to open them up. Pop in a little vegan butter and fluff up the potato, then top with the tuna mix and scatter over some vegan cheese, if desired.

TIP
The filling works so well as a chickpea tuna melt with thick sliced fresh bread and vegan cheese. Or try it as a pasta bake by adding soy cream, mixing with pasta tubes and baking in the oven.

Broccoli and tofu are two protein powerhouses that are the perfect food for a workout week. This dish is great to get in all of those macros while not ignoring your taste buds.

# Broccoli bowl

SERVES 2

1 head of broccoli, cut into florets
100g (½ cup) bulgur wheat
Olive oil, for frying
1 tbsp walnuts
1 tbsp pumpkin seeds
1 x 400g block of firm tofu, cut into cubes
2 tbsp hoisin sauce
2 garlic cloves, very finely chopped
2 spring onions, thinly sliced

Cook the broccoli florets in boiling salted water for 3-4 minutes until tender. Drain, reserving the cooking liquid.

Add the bulgur wheat to a large bowl and pour in 250ml (1 cup) of the reserved broccoli cooking water.

In a frying pan, warm a little oil, add the walnuts and pumpkin seeds and toast until lightly browned and fragrant. Remove from the pan and set aside.

Meanwhile, coat the tofu in the hoisin sauce and quickly fry it in the pan over a medium heat until golden brown.

Add the garlic to the puffed-up bulgur wheat and fluff up with a fork. Divide the bulgur wheat and broccoli florets between two serving bowls. Add the tofu and sprinkle over the seeds, walnuts and spring onions.

This warm salad, with its crispy, cheesy, nutty croutons, is as good as a salad gets. Serve to friends and family and wait for the positive feedback. Before you know it, it will be the dish they are requesting at lunches or asking you to bring to get-togethers and BBQs.

# Asparagus salad

SERVES 2

1 red pepper, deseeded and cut into thick slices
5 tbsp olive oil
Pinch of coarse sea salt
10 thin asparagus stems
250g baby plum or cherry tomatoes
Pinch of sugar
2 garlic cloves
1 small courgette, thinly sliced
2 tbsp (½ cup) nutritional yeast
1 small ciabatta, torn into bite-size pieces
Black pepper, to taste
Rocket leaves
150g bag baby leaf and herb salad (optional)
2 tbsp balsamic vinegar

Preheat the oven to 180°C/160°C Fan/350°F/gas 4. Put the red pepper slices in a baking tray, drizzle with 4 tablespoons of the olive oil and sprinkle with coarse salt and bake for 20 minutes.

Cut the asparagus into 2cm (¾in) long pieces and add to the peppers in the baking tray along with the whole cherry tomatoes. Sprinkle with the sugar and cook for a further 10 minutes.

Meanwhile, heat the remaining tablespoon of olive oil in a pan over a low heat, then add the garlic and cook until softened.

Add the courgette slices to the pan, sprinkle with half of the nutritional yeast and cook for 15 minutes over a low heat. Remove the courgette slices using a slotted spoon and set aside.

Mop up the oil and yeast from the pan with the ciabatta chunks, then season with black pepper and cook on the grill under on a low heat for 5 minutes until browned.

In a large salad bowl, toss together the rocket, salad leaves, if using, and balsamic vinegar with all the roasted ingredients. Scatter over the ciabatta croutons to serve.

This is a recipe I created while travelling through Italy. It features so many flavours that pair perfectly with farro wheat. A delicious dish that is packed full of goodness.

# Warm Italian salad

SERVES 2

150g (1 cup) cherry
   tomatoes, cut into
   quarters
130g (1 cup) cooked
   artichokes in oil
2 tbsp capers
4 tbsp pitted black olives
6 runner beans, chopped
2 tbsp olive oil
Pinch of salt and pepper
1 tbsp (¼ cup) nutritional
   yeast
80g (½ cup) farro wheat
Oregano leaves, to garnish
Basil leaves, to garnish
   (optional)

Preheat the oven to 180°C/160°C Fan/350°F/gas 4.

Put the tomatoes, artichokes, capers, olives and runner beans in a baking dish, add the oil and mix together, then season with salt and nutritional yeast and cook in the oven for 15 minutes.

Meanwhile, boil 250ml (1 cup) salted water in a pan, tip in the farro wheat and simmer for 30 minutes. Once cooked, drain, then tip the farro into a serving dish, and mix in the baked vegetables.

Serve garnished with the oregano leaves and basil, if you like.

A green bowl of goodness. This is a fresh combination of food that is perfect for using up leftovers such as cooked pasta.

# Green pea bowl

SERVES 2

110g (1 cup) fresh or
    defrosted frozen peas
Handful of mint leaves
1 red chilli, finely chopped
2 tbsp olive oil
½ courgette, thinly sliced
200g (1 cup) cooked pasta
    tubes (70g dried weight)
15g (½ cup) chopped basil,
    plus a sprig to garnish
2 tsp Vegan pesto (see
    page 40)
1 tbsp pine nuts, to garnish
Pinch of salt and pepper

Combine all of the ingredients in a large bowl and toss to coat everything in the pesto.

Sprinkle over the pine nuts. Garnish with a sprig of basil and season with salt and pepper to taste.

This is a salad that won't leave you unsatisfied. Sweet potato, quinoa and peppered cashew cheese are the perfect combination. You can use up leftover sweet potato here, or cook it fresh and add it warm.

# Sweet potato salad

SERVES 2

120g (¾ cup) quinoa

2 handfuls of peppery salad leaves

1 baked sweet potato, peeled and cut into cubes

155g (1 cup) edamame beans

2 tbsp sunflower seeds

4 tbsp Peppered cashew cheese sauce (see page 52)

Mint leaves, torn, to garnish

Rinse the quinoa in a sieve under cold running water – this removes some of the bitter flavour from the outside of the quinoa and makes it taste a little less earthy when cooked. Tip it into a pan then add double the amount of salted water on top and stir the grains. Over a high heat, bring the water to the boil, then reduce the heat to a simmer and cook for 10–15 minutes, or until tender and the liquid has been absorbed. Tip into a bowl and fluff up the grains with a fork.

Place a handful of salad leaves into each individual serving bowl, then add the baked sweet potato cubes and the edamame beans. Sprinkle over the sunflower seeds and top the potato with the peppered cashew cheese sauce.

Serve garnished with the torn mint leaves.

TIP
To bake a sweet potato, pierce the skin several times, wrap it in tinfoil then bake in the oven at 180°C/160°C Fan/350°F/gas 4 for 45 minutes until cooked but still firm.

Creamy mushroom tagliatelle is one of my most-viewed videos on Instagram. This is a quick and easy dish that will become one of your go-to favourites.

# Mushroom tagliatelle

SERVES 4

280g tagliatelle
Drizzle of olive oil
250g chestnut mushrooms,
    sliced
2 tbsp garlic purée
2 tsp smoked paprika
1 tsp onion powder
2 handfuls of spinach,
    roughly chopped
200ml (⅘ cups) soy cream

Cook the tagliatelle in a pan of boiling water until al dente, following the packet instructions. Drain and set to one side.

Heat a little oil in a pan over a medium heat, add the mushrooms and cook for 5 minutes. Stir in the garlic purée, smoked paprika and onion powder and stir occasionally until the mushrooms are cooked through.

Stir in the spinach and soy cream. Tip in the pasta, toss to coat in the sauce and serve immediately.

Cottage pie is a food full of memories for me. It's a really hearty dish that was a staple at home, so I wanted to include my own vegan version here. Mustard mash is a lovely addition and will come out crispy, crunchy and full of that subtle mustardy heat.

# Cottage pie

SERVES 4

*For the mash*
2 potatoes, peeled and
    chopped
1 teaspoon English mustard
1 teaspoon soy cream or
    plant-based butter

*For the cottage pie filling*
Olive oil, for frying
1 onion, diced
2 tbsp garlic purée or
    3 garlic cloves, finely
    chopped
450g (2 cups) soy mince
1 carrot, finely chopped
110g (1 cup) frozen peas
1 tsp dried rosemary
1 tsp dried thyme
2 tbsp gravy granules
Salt and pepper, to taste

Add the potatoes to a pan of boiling water and cook for 25 minutes. Once cooked, drain and mash with the mustard and soy cream or butter.

Meanwhile, heat a little oil in a deep pan over a low heat, add the onion and garlic and sauté for 5 minutes until translucent. Tip in the mince, carrot, peas, rosemary and thyme and fry for 5–10 minutes over a medium heat. Stir in the gravy granules with 500ml (2 cups) boiling water, then leave to simmer over a low heat for 10 minutes until the sauce has thickened.

Preheat the oven to 180°C/160°C Fan/350°F/gas 4. Transfer the mince to a baking dish, cover with the mash and cook in the oven for 30 minutes. Serve piping hot with your choice of greens.

Stuffed peppers are great, but protein-packed peppers are another level. Pack in your protein but don't compromise on flavour.

# Protein-packed peppers

SERVES 2

170g (1 cup) quinoa
Pinch of salt
Olive oil, for frying
1 onion, finely chopped
3 garlic cloves, finely
    chopped
1 courgette, thinly sliced
1 x 400g block of firm tofu,
    cut into cubes
1 tsp smoked paprika
1 tsp dried oregano
Juice of ½ lemon
4 red peppers
Vegan cheese, grated
    (optional)

Rinse the quinoa in a sieve under running water. Pour 500ml (2 cups) cold water into a pan, add a little salt and the quinoa and bring to the boil. Reduce to a simmer and cook for 12 minutes.

While the quinoa cooks, add a little oil to a pan and gently fry the onion and garlic. After a few minutes, add the courgette slices, the tofu cubes, smoked paprika and oregano and gently stir until the quinoa is cooked.

Once cooked, fluff up the quinoa with a fork and add to the pan with the tofu. Squeeze over the lemon juice and lightly fry for 5 more minutes.

Preheat the oven to 170°C/150°C Fan/325°F/gas 3.

Cut around the stalk on each of the peppers to create a little lid and set aside. Tap out any seeds, then take a thin slice from the base to ensure the pepper can stand up straight. Fill with the quinoa and tofu mixture, and, if you like, top with some vegan cheese. Replace the lids and place the peppers on a baking tray. Bake in the oven for 30–40 minutes until bubbling and golden.

Cauliflower steaks are a crunchy, healthy alternative to the meat option that are really growing in popularity among vegans and non-vegans, too. You can buy them ready cut in some supermarkets, but you can easily make your own for a fraction of the price.

## Cauliflower steaks

SERVES 2

2 heads of cauliflower

1 tbsp olive oil, plus extra
   for drizzling

1 tbsp tahini

2 tbsp lemon juice

1 tbsp garlic purée or 2
   finely chopped garlic
   cloves

1 tsp smoked paprika flakes
   (optional)

8 tomatoes on the vine

150g (1 cup) green beans

Salt and pepper, to taste

2 tbsp sunflower or
   pumpkin seeds (optional)

*For the sweet potato mash*

2 sweet potatoes, peeled
   and diced

A little cashew milk and
   vegan butter, for mashing

First prepare the cauliflower steaks. Cut 2 slices from the centre of each cauliflower head, roughly 1cm (½in) thick or just under. (Save the rest of the cauliflower to roast for your next meal.)

In a small bowl, mix the olive oil, tahini, lemon juice and garlic and carefully brush this on the cauliflower steaks. Lay the cauliflower steaks on a baking tray lined with baking parchment, sprinkle with the smoked paprika flakes, if using, and roast for 15 minutes.

Take the steaks out of the oven and add the tomatoes on their vines and green beans and drizzle with olive oil. Season with salt and then turn over the steaks carefully with a spatula. Return to the oven and bake for another 15 minutes.

Meanwhile, cook the sweet potatoes in a pan of boiling water for 5 minutes until tender. Drain, then return to the pan and use a masher to mash the potatoes (you can add a little cashew milk and vegan butter, but only a little at a time as the mash will thin out quickly and become runny).

When the cauliflower steaks are ready, spoon the sweet potato mash on to the centre of each plate and use the back of the spoon to flatten it down into a dish shape. Remove the steaks from the oven and place two on top of each pile of mash. Add the green beans and tomatoes to the side of the plate. Sprinkle over the seeds, if using, and eat!

This classic Italian peasant dish is full of flavour and nutrients. I love dishes like this that are simple to eat and full of goodness; it is traditionally celebrated for its cheap and filling nature, which is exactly why I celebrate it too.

## Pasta e fagioli

SERVES 4

Olive oil, for cooking
and drizzling
1 onion, diced
3 garlic cloves, finely
chopped
1 carrot, chopped
2 celery sticks, chopped
½ x 400g tin tomatoes
½ x 400g tin green lentils
1 x 400g tin haricot beans
2 sprigs of rosemary, leaves
very finely chopped
2 tbsp liquid vegetable
stock
Pinch of garlic pepper
Pinch of onion salt
½ tsp smoked paprika
2 pinches of dried parsley
200g (2 cups) pasta shells

Heat some oil in a pan over a low heat and fry the onion, garlic, carrot and celery for 5 minutes, stirring occasionally until browned.

Add the tomatoes, green lentils and haricot beans, including all of their juices, to the pan and stir together. Stir in most of the rosemary along with the vegetable stock, garlic pepper, onion salt, paprika and a pinch of dried parsley. Tip in the pasta, pour in 1 litre (4 cups) boiling water and simmer for 15 minutes until it has softened but is still slightly firm to bite.

Serve with a drizzle of olive oil, a pinch of dried parsley and the remaining chopped rosemary scattered over.

Italian and Mexican foods are two of my favourites, so I thought I'd try pairing delicious spicy Mexican flavours with some perfectly cooked linguini. Turned out to be a match made in heaven.

# Linguini fusion

SERVES 2

150g dried linguini

Oil, for frying

3 red chillies, deseeded and finely chopped

3 shallots, thinly sliced

3 garlic cloves, finely chopped

200g mushrooms, sliced

2 limes, 1 cut into wedges

Large bunch of coriander, roughly chopped

150ml (⅔ cup) vegan soy cream

Cook the pasta in a pan of boiling water following the packet instructions. Drain.

Heat some oil in a pan over a low heat, then add the chillies, shallots and garlic.

After a few minutes of frying, add the mushrooms, the juice of 1 of the limes and half of the coriander, then cook for 5–10 minutes, stirring occasionally. Pour in the soy cream and stir to combine.

Tip the cooked pasta into the sauce and toss to coat.

Serve scattered with the remaining coriander and with lime wedges for squeezing over.

A classic dish with a vegan twist. Sausage and lentil casserole is perfect for a family dinner. Use your favourite vegan sausages or try adding stuffing mix to the dish instead (see tip).

# Sausage and lentil casserole

SERVES 4

2 tbsp olive oil

1 onion, chopped

2 garlic cloves, crushed

4 carrots, chopped

1 tsp smoked paprika

1 x 400g tin chopped
    tomatoes

1 x 400g tin green lentils

4 large potatoes, quartered

400ml (1⅔ cups) vegetable
    stock

1–2 bay leaves

80g (½ cup) farro wheat

8 vegan sausages (try Linda
    McCartney)

Chopped parsley, to
    garnish

Heat a little of the oil in a casserole dish or large pan. Add the onion and soften for a few minutes, then add the garlic and carrots and sprinkle with the paprika. After 5 minutes of cooking add the tomatoes, lentils and their juice, potatoes and stock and stir to combine. Pop in the bay leaves and simmer for 10 minutes.

Remove the bay leaves and stir in the farro wheat, then place the sausages on top and simmer for another 15 minutes until warmed through.

Serve piping hot, scattered with chopped parsley.

TIP
Although vegan sausages are now widely available, if you struggle to get hold of some, you can just make little balls from stuffing mix and add them to the stew like dumplings.

Sag aloo is a real vegan go-to when going for a curry, but it is also really easy to recreate at home. This spicy spinach dish is healthy and filling and can be served as a side or enjoyed by itself. Save some for the Stuffed sag aloo bread (see page 171) and you are in for a treat.

## Sag aloo

SERVES 4

2 tbsp sunflower oil
1 onion, sliced
2 garlic cloves, sliced
1 tbsp chopped fresh
    ginger
500g potatoes, cut into
    cubes
1 large red chilli, halved,
    deseeded and thinly
    sliced
½ tsp black mustard seeds
½ tsp cumin seeds
½ tsp ground turmeric
½ tsp salt
250g spinach leaves
Handful of coriander,
    roughly chopped

Heat the oil in a large pan, add the onion, garlic and ginger and fry for about 3 minutes. Stir in the potatoes, chilli, spices and salt and continue cooking and stirring for 5 minutes more.

Add a splash of water, cover and cook for 8–10 minutes. Check the potatoes are ready by spearing a cube with the point of a knife, and if they are, add the spinach and let it wilt.

Take off the heat and serve garnished with the coriander.

Biscuits are basically American scones, which are often served with mash, a flavourful gravy and greens. This dish is built on a classic but is really one of a kind. Cognac mushroom gravy is the perfect partner for a fluffy biscuit. Serve with mangetout or green beans.

## Savoury 'biscuits' with mushroom gravy

SERVES 2

3 tsp vegan butter

250g (2 cups) mushrooms, thinly sliced

25ml cognac

3 tsp black pepper

4 sprigs of thyme

2 garlic cloves, finely chopped

2 shallots, thinly sliced

2 tbsp plain flour

200ml (⅘ cups) veg stock

200ml (⅘ cups) plant-based milk, plus 2 tbsp

2 medium potatoes, peeled and cut into chunks

1 tbsp wholegrain mustard

*For the biscuits*

250g plain flour, plus extra for dusting

2 tsp baking powder

1 tsp sugar

1 tsp sea salt

75g unsalted vegan butter

100ml (scant ½ cup) plant-based milk or soy cream

Preheat the oven to 220°C/200°C Fan/425°F/gas 7.

First make the biscuits. In a large bowl, combine the flour, baking powder, sugar and salt. Add the butter and mix it in with the tips of your fingers until you have the consistency of breadcrumbs. Slowly pour in the milk or cream, mixing gently until everything comes together as a dough.

On a lightly dusted surface, tip out and knead the dough lightly, pressing and folding it about 10 times. Roll the dough 5cm (2in) thick, then use a floured cutter to cut out 8–9 biscuits. Bake for 10–12 minutes until the biscuits are golden brown.

Next, get started on the gravy. Melt 2 teaspoons of the vegan butter in a large pan and cook the mushrooms along with the cognac, black pepper, thyme, garlic and shallots. After a few minutes, stir in the flour, then pour in the veg stock and plant-based milk and simmer for 20 minutes until the sauce has thickened.

Meanwhile, cook the potatoes in a pan of boiling water until tender. Drain, then return to the pan and mash with the remaining teaspoon of vegan butter and the 2 tablespoons of plant milk to a creamy consistency. Stir through the mustard.

Place 2 biscuits on each serving plate, along with some mash and mangetout. Pour the mushroom gravy over the mash and biscuits, and serve any extra gravy in a jug on the side.

Roasted new potatoes are sweet, crispy potato goodness and these paired with garlic aioli is a winning combination. Great with a roasted dinner or as a side dish. You can also try making fries the same way. Delicious.

# Roasted new potatoes with garlic aioli

SERVES 4 AS A SIDE

500g new potatoes
5 tbsp olive oil, plus extra
  for drizzling
2 tsp smoked paprika
  flakes
1 tbsp dried oregano
½ tsp smoked salt

*For the garlic aioli*
125ml (½ cup) chilled
  unsweetened soy milk
  or soy cream
1 tsp apple cider vinegar
½ tbsp lemon juice
½ tsp maple syrup
½ tsp dried mustard
  powder
½ tsp salt
3 garlic cloves, finely
  chopped
250ml (1 cup) olive oil

Preheat the oven to 180°C/160°C Fan/350°F/gas 4.

Add the potatoes to a large bowl and cover with the oive oil, then mix to ensure they are all coated.

Place on a baking tray and dust them evenly with the paprika, oregano and smoked salt. Bake for 20 minutes.

While the potatoes are baking, make the garlic aioli. Add all of the ingredients apart from the oil, to a high-speed blender (preferably one that you can pour ingredients into the top of while it's on), then blend on high speed until combined. Lower the speed and pour in the oil a little bit at a time – the mixture should slowly start to thicken. Once all of the oil is added, continue to blend for another minute. If you like, feel free to add you choice of chopped fresh herbs (chives work well). Set aside until potatoes are ready, or transfer to a jar, seal and store in the fridge where it will keep for 1 week.

Remove the potatoes from the oven and use a potato masher or fork to crush each one just enough so that the skin breaks in a few places. Drizzle with a little extra oil, then return to the oven and bake for another 20 minutes. Serve hot and crispy, with the aioli on the side.

# 02

# What Vegans Eat

—

# With Their Gang

# COOKING FOR A CROWD

## CROWD-PLEASING CLASSICS

Caponata

Rainbow slaw

Fresh potato salad

Coconut, chickpea and spinach curry

Chickpea chow

Squash madras

Garlic and coriander naan

Pizza dough

Mexican pizza

Chilli non carne

Garlic and herb tear and share

Poppy seed onion rings

Tater tots

Onion bhaji burger

Walnut and potato tacos

Hasselback squash

Zucca al forno

Sundried tomato, red pepper and garlic dip

---

## SPECIAL OCCASIONS

Zeviostrone

Open lasagne

Gourmet gratin

Thai green greens

Asparagus risotto

Gnocchi

White wine and pesto gnocchi

A traditional fried aubergine dish that is often served on bruschetta.
I first experimented with this dish when I cooked for some locals
while travelling through Tuscany – I served it then with tagliatelle,
but you can eat it how you like.

# Caponata

SERVES 4

Olive oil, for frying
1 large aubergine, cut into
    1cm dice
Pinch of salt
1 tsp dried oregano
1 shallot, thinly sliced
2 garlic cloves, thinly sliced
1 celery stick, thinly sliced
2 large ripe tomatoes,
    roughly chopped
2 tbsp red wine vinegar
2 tbsp raisins
2 tbsp pine nuts
1 tbsp salted capers
½ tsp sugar
½ bunch (15g) flat-leaf
    parsley, chopped

Add a large glug of olive oil to a deep pan and heat over a low heat. Add the aubergine chunks to the pan with the salt and oregano and cook for roughly 15 minutes until softened. Remove the aubergine from the pan and set aside on a plate.

In the same pan, fry the shallots and garlic over a low heat for a few minutes until softened. Now add the celery, tomatoes and red wine vinegar and cook for a few minutes until some of the juice has evaporated and the tomatoes are beginning to break up. Return the aubergine to the pan along with the raisins, pine nuts, capers and sugar and simmer for 30 minutes.

Serve on bruschetta, paired with pasta or even on its own, scattered with parsley.

You've heard it – eat the rainbow! This tasty slaw makes that so easy to do. It's great on burgers, perfect for picnics and brilliant at a buffet. You need to slice the cabbage really thinly here – the thinner the better! See photo overleaf.

# Rainbow slaw

SERVES 4 AS A SIDE

¼ white cabbage, sliced very thinly

⅛ red cabbage, sliced very thinly

1 carrot, grated

5 tbsp raisins

1 tsp smoked paprika, plus extra to garnish

125ml (½ cup) vegan mayo

2 tbsp apple cider vinegar

Handful of dill, chopped

Put the white and red cabbage in a large mixing bowl, then add the grated carrot and raisins and mix them together with your hands. Sprinkle with the smoked paprika and add in the mayo and apple cider vinegar, using a spoon to combine. Add the chopped dill and mix again.

Serve sprinkled with a little extra paprika on top in a large sharing dish or in smaller side dishes.

TIP
This recipe is best when made a few hours ahead of time or stored overnight, as the raisins will soak up some of the moisture and rehydrate slightly, and the cabbage will absorb the moisture of the mayo and apple cider vinegar and the flavour of the smoked paprika.

Crowd-pleasing classics

If you have ever grown your own potatoes you'll know that you go from no potatoes to more potatoes than you know what to do with really quickly. When my oldest friend Will gave me a glut of potatoes from his allotment, this is the dish I created. It goes perfectly with Rainbow slaw – see page 107 for the recipe.

# Fresh potato salad

SERVES 4

800g new potatoes, cut into quarters
110g (1 cup) fresh petit pois
3 spring onions, thinly sliced
2 long shallots, very thinly sliced
3 chillies, deseeded and thinly sliced
60ml (¼ cup) olive oil
Handful of cress
Salt and pepper, to taste

Bring a pan of water to the boil, add the new potatoes, bring to the boil and then simmer for 10 minutes.

Put the peas, spring onions, shallots and chillies into a large bowl. Drain the potatoes and add them to the bowl while still piping hot. Pour over the olive oil and mix to coat all the ingredients evenly.

Sprinkle the cress on top, season with salt and black pepper and serve while still warm.

This dish is close to my heart. It was taught to me in traditional style by my good friend Anita Kudhail. I have adapted it slightly to make it as easy as possible but this curry is now the main request I get at all family parties and events. A real crowd-pleaser. Thank you, Anita!

# Coconut, chickpea and spinach curry

SERVES 4–6

1 tbsp coconut oil
2 onions, finely chopped
2 tbsp mustard seeds
1 tsp ground cumin
1 tsp curry powder
1 tsp garam masala
1 tsp ground turmeric
2 green chillies, finely chopped
2 tomatoes, roughly chopped
½ x 400g tin tomatoes
2 tbsp garlic purée
1 tbsp ginger purée
2 x 400g tins chickpeas
½ x 400g tin coconut milk
3 tbsp desiccated coconut
60ml (¼ cup) maple syrup
250g spinach leaves
Small bunch of coriander (30g), chopped

Heat the coconut oil in a wok or large pan and add the onions, mustard seeds, cumin, curry powder, garam masala and turmeric and stir. Cook for a few minutes until the onions have caramelised, then add the chillies, fresh and tinned tomatoes, garlic and ginger purées and stir everything to combine.

Tip one tin of chickpeas into a blender with the liquid and pulse to blend, then add to the pan. Drain the second tin of chickpeas, and add to the pan. Simmer for 20 minutes.

Stir in the coconut milk, desiccated coconut and maple syrup with the spinach and simmer for a further 15 minutes to thicken.

Stir in half the coriander, reserving the rest to use as a garnish.

This dish is an adaptation of the classic Indian dish bunny chow, a hollowed-out loaf that workers would fill with leftover curry to take to work for lunch.

# Chickpea chow

SERVES 2 AS A SMALL LUNCH OR SNACK

2 crusty cob rolls
500ml (2 cups) leftover Coconut, chickpea, and spinach curry (see opposite)
Handful of coriander, chopped
1 red chilli, thinly sliced (optional)

Roughly one-fifth of the way down the cob roll, cut across to take off the 'lid'. Set the top to one side then use your fingers to scoop out the soft bread inside, keeping the bread in a bowl.

Carefully spoon the curry into the roll and scatter over a little coriander and the red chilli, if using. Pop the top back on and serve the roll with the soft bread on the side for dipping.

Butternut squash and red peppers are sweet and succulent; madras is fiery and flavoursome. Together they complement each other perfectly. Whether it's curry night or you just fancy some spice, this is a must! Try it with Garlic and coriander naan (see page 114).

## Squash madras

SERVES 4

Drizzle of olive oil
½ butternut squash, cut into cubes
3 tbsp madras paste
1 tbsp garlic purée
1 tsp ground turmeric
1 large onion, roughly sliced
1 red pepper, deseeded and sliced
3 handfuls of spinach
125ml (½ cup) coconut milk

Drizzle the olive oil into a frying pan set over a medium heat, add the cubes of butternut squash, madras paste, garlic purée, turmeric, onion, and red pepper to the pan, stirring all of the ingredients together to coat them in the paste. Leave to cook for 10 minutes.

Add the spinach and leave to wilt for 5 minutes before stirring the mixture together.

Pour in the coconut milk, stir, and simmer for 15 minutes until the squash is cooked through and the curry is fragrant. Remove from the heat and serve in deep bowls.

Curry night is not complete without naan bread. This garlic and coriander naan is the perfect accompaniment for any curry (see pages 110 and 112). See photo on previous page.

# Garlic and coriander naan

SERVES 4

125ml (½ cup) warm water
1 tsp dried yeast (if using fast-action, cut rise time in half)
1 tbsp maple or agave syrup
¾ tsp baking powder
350g (2 ½ cups) plain flour, plus extra for dusting
1 tsp fine sea salt
60ml (¼ cup) plant-based milk
3 garlic cloves, very finely chopped
Bunch of coriander, chopped
2 tbsp olive oil
1 tbsp garlic purée

Put the warm water, yeast, syrup and baking powder into a jug and mix together to activate.

In a large bowl, combine the flour and salt – this is important, as if the yeast is mixed directly with the salt it will die and limit the rise.

Pour the wet yeast mix and the milk into the flour and stir gently to combine. Then add the garlic and half the coriander.

Tip out the dough on to a lightly floured work surface and knead for 5–10 minutes until you have a smooth dough. Split into 4 balls, press each one flat and allow to prove for 30 minutes.

Brush the dough with oil and garlic purée.

Heat the oil in a frying pan over a medium heat. When hot add the naans one at a time and cook for 3 minutes until they begin to bubble. Turn over to cook the other side.

Once cooked, brush with a little oil and sprinkle with the remaining chopped coriander.

A classic pizza dough that you can use as the base for any magical toppings you like, or you can simply drizzle with olive oil and sprinkle with garlic for an easy garlic bread.

# Pizza dough

SERVES 2

1 tbsp granulated sugar
7g dried fast-action yeast
200ml (⅘ cup) warm water
    250g (1⅔ cups) plain flour,
    plus extra for dusting
50g semolina, plus extra
    for dusting
1 tsp salt
Drizzle of oil

Mix together the sugar, yeast and warm water in a jug.

Put the flour, semolina and salt into a large mixing bowl and stir together. Make a well in the centre of the flour mixture and pour in the liquid. Using a spatula, mix together until combined. Dust a work surface with flour and tip the dough on to it. Begin to knead the dough with one hand by pressing and folding the mixture continuously for a few minutes. Then take the mixture in the palm of one hand and begin to push the mixture away, stretching it with the other hand. When the dough is starts to tear, fold the mixture back on itself and turn it 90 degrees, then do this roughly 20 times. This process is important to stretch the dough and form gluten bonds to improve the rise.

Now form into a ball shape. Grease a clean bowl with olive oil, add the dough and cover with cling film or a wet towel and leave to prove for between 30 minutes and 2 hours.

Preheat the oven to 180°C/160°C Fan/350°F/gas 4.

Tip the dough out on to a work surface dusted with flour and begin to stretch the dough with your fingers from the inside out, gently stretching it to 30–35cm (12–14 in).

Transfer the pizza base to a baking tray and top with your favourite toppings, then bake in the oven for 15 minutes.

I first made this Mexican pizza for my good friend and world-class DJ, Benj, while I interviewed him. It was so popular I had to make another immediately, so I couldn't not share it with you here! See photo on previous page.

## Mexican pizza

SERVES 2

1 portion of Pizza dough
    (see page 115)
100g vegan cheese, grated
½ portion of Marinara
    sauce (see page 75)
120g beans from Dirty
    beans on toast (see page
    32), or use tinned black
    beans in a chilli sauce
Handful of nachos (any
    flavour)
3 jalapeños, thinly sliced
1 avocado, cut in half and
    stoned
2 rocket chillies, deseeded
    and finely chopped
Pinch of salt
Juice of ¼ lime
Vegan mayo or sour cream,
    to serve

Preheat the oven to 180°C/160°C Fan/350°F/gas 4.

Start by preparing the pizza base and sauce. Spread the sauce evenly over the base and sprinkle with the grated vegan cheese.

Add the beans, a tablespoon at a time, and spread them over the pizza. Next, crush the nachos slightly then scatter them over. Top with the jalapeño slices. Bake in the oven for 15 minutes.

Scoop out the avocado flesh and mush it up in a bowl using a fork, then add the chillies. Sprinkle with the salt and lime juice and set aside.

Once the pizza is cooked, spoon on the avocado, in dollops or spread evenly. Drizzle with vegan mayo or sour cream. Cut into slices and enjoy!

Chilli is about sweet, smoky, spicy flavours. This is a soy mince chilli with tons of flavour and is served with a sweet peanut butter dollop for extra flavour and texture.

# Chilli non carne

SERVES 4

Drizzle of olive oil
1 onion, finely chopped
1 red pepper, deseeded
    and finely chopped
500g vegan soy mince
1 tbsp garlic purée
2 tbsp smoky seasoning
2 tbsp BBQ sauce
1 x 600g jar passata
1 x 400g tin black beans,
    drained
2 sweet potatoes, peeled
    and cubed
2 chillies, deseeded and
    finely chopped
2 limes
4 tsp peanut butter
Handful of coriander,
    chopped

Heat a drizzle of olive oil in a large pan. Add the onion, red pepper and soy mince and fry for 5 minutes over a low heat.

Stir in the garlic purée then add the smoky seasoning to the pan and stir to completely coat. Pour in the BBQ sauce, passata, black beans, sweet potato cubes and chillies and stir to combine, then cook over a low heat for 30 minutes until the vegetables have softened and the sauce has thickened. Squeeze the juice of 1 lime over the chilli.

Serve in deep bowls. Add a quarter of the second lime and a teaspoon of peanut butter to each bowl, and scatter with chopped coriander.

Tear and share is perfect for get-togethers or movie nights. It is so simple to make but is a really impressive-looking dish. Make this when you're having company over, as when left alone with it you might not be able to resist eating the whole thing! Perfect with pesto and tapenade for dipping.

# Garlic and herb tear and share

SERVES 8

500g plain flour, plus extra for dusting

2 pinches of onion salt, plus extra for dusting

7g dried fast-action yeast

1 tbsp sugar

2 tbsp garlic purée, plus extra for brushing

1 tsp dried basil, plus extra for dusting

1 tsp dried oregano, plus extra for dusting

Drizzle of olive oil, plus extra for brushing

Put the flour in a large bowl and add the onion salt. In a separate bowl, combine 300ml (1¼ cups) water with the yeast and sugar. Make a well in the centre of the flour mixture and pour in the water and yeast mix, then begin to bind together with a spatula. Add the garlic purée, basil and oregano and continue to mix together to form a ball of dough.

Dust a work surface with flour and tip the dough out on to it. Roll the mixture in the flour and begin to knead by taking the palm of your left hand and using it to secure the dough in place, then pushing the dough away with your right hand, stretching it and folding it back on itself, turning and repeating this process 20–30 times.

Drizzle a little olive oil into a clean large bowl, put the dough in, cover with cling film or a wet tea towel and leave for 1 hour to prove.

Preheat the oven to 180°C/160°C Fan/350°F/gas 4. Tip the dough on to a dusted work surface, roll it into a sausage shape and divide into 3 equal pieces. Roll these pieces into three long sausage shapes, then take the ends and begin to plait the pieces together by folding one outer piece in between the other two pieces, then taking the outer piece from the opposite side and folding this in between the other two. Keep repeating this process until the plait is complete.

Once finished, transfer the plait to an ovenproof frying pan or round cake tin, spiralling to make a large circular bun shape. Before placing the bread in the oven, brush the top of the bread all over with a little olive oil and garlic purée and sprinkle with onion salt, basil and oregano. Bake in the oven for 25 minutes, then allow to cool slightly before eating.

TIP
The tear and share bread recipe will also work as dough balls! Why not try splitting into balls about half the size of a golf ball and place them on a baking tray. Glaze and season as above but cut the cooking time down to 20 minutes and you have the perfect sharing option for get togethers.

Onion rings make a crunchy side that's super-satisfying. These poppy seed onion rings have some extra crunch and are delicious served with sandwiches and burgers – and Tater tots! (See recipe overleaf).

## Poppy seed onion rings

SERVES 4

1 tsp poppy seeds
125g (1 cup) plain flour
    (unbleached is best)
¼ tsp bicarbonate of soda
¼ tsp baking powder
Pinch of salt and pepper
250ml (1 cup) vegan beer
    (Stella Artois, Budweiser,
    Beck's, Carlsberg, San
    Miguel, Heineken)
2 tbsp vegetable oil
1 tbsp apple cider vinegar
Oil, for deep-frying
3 onions, thinly sliced

In a large bowl, combine all the dry ingredients. In a measuring jug, combine all the wet ingredients, then pour them into the bowl with the flour mixture slowly, stirring all the time to make a smooth batter.

Heat the oil in a deep frying pan or wok until very hot – you can test it is ready by dropping a piece of onion in it; it should sizzle.

Dip the onion slices into the batter and coat, shaking off any excess, then gently place them straight into the hot oil – stand back to avoid the hot oil spitting at you. Cook for a minute or so until golden brown, watching them all the time so that they don't burn. Using a slotted spoon, scoop out the onion rings and transfer to a plate lined with kitchen paper to absorb some of the excess hot oil. Serve immediately!

Making your own tater tots is a must! They're so simple but so satisfying. A lot of ready-made tater tots contain eggs or milk, so give these a try and you'll never need to mess around reading labels. See the photo on previous page.

# Tater tots

3 medium potatoes, peeled
1 tbsp plain flour
1 tsp smoked paprika
1 tsp dried oregano
1 tsp onion salt
50ml oil

Cook the potatoes, whole, in a pan of boiling water for 10 minutes. Drain and set aside to cool for 3 minutes until cool enough to handle. Grate the potatoes on the large hole of a grater into a large bowl.

Add the flour to the grated potato, along with the smoked paprika, oregano and onion salt. Stir to coat the potato in the seasonings.

Preheat the oven to 180°C/160°C Fan/350°F/gas 4.

Using a tablespoon, spoon the mixture on to a perforated baking sheet in little piles, then flatten with the back of the spoon. Brush the tots with a thin coating of your choice of oil and bake in the oven for 40 minutes. Check that they are crispy and golden brown, if not, pop them back in the oven for a few more minutes.

Allow to cool slightly before enjoying with your favourite dips.

Onion bhajis are a crispy ball of goodness. Drop that on a bun with some rainbow slaw and we are in business! I first cooked this dish for my friend and rapper, Zeo, while interviewing him and he made it himself a lot after that so I guess he liked it. You can also just make the bhajis as a starter or side for a curry. Delicious!

# Onion bhaji burger

SERVES 4

80g (⅔ cup) gram
   (chickpea) flour
1 tsp ground cumin
1 tsp ground coriander
1 tsp ground turmeric
2 pinches of salt
Bunch of coriander
2 chillies, deseeded and
   finely chopped
1 large onion, thinly sliced
100ml (scant ½ cup)
   sparkling water
Drizzle of vegetable oil

*To serve*
4 buns, cut in half
Rainbow slaw (see page 107)

Add the gram (chickpea) flour to a jug, then add the cumin, coriander, turmeric, salt, coriander and chillies and stir to combine. Drop the onion slices into the mixture and coat them in the spiced flour. Pour in the sparkling water, a little at a time, and stir to mix to a smooth, thick batter. Leave the onion slices to soak for 15 minutes.

Add the vegetable oil to a frying pan set over a medium heat. Scoop out the onion rings and batter using a ladle or large spoon and space 4–5 patties in the pan, then shallow-fry the bhajis, turning them after a few minutes, and cook until crispy and golden brown on both sides.

Put the bhaji pattie on the bottom half of a bun, top with rainbow slaw and the bun lid and serve.

Walnuts are full of goodness, and when paired with fried grated potato they add a lovely crunchy texture to these tacos. Spice, sweetness and tangy lime – what's not to like?

# Walnut and potato tacos

SERVES 2

3 tbsp olive oil

1 large potato, grated and patted dry with a tea towel

3 garlic cloves, finely chopped

1 onion, finely chopped

2 chillies, finely chopped

200g walnuts, blended or finely chopped

1 tsp smoked paprika

½ tsp onion salt

4 tbsp BBQ sauce

2 tbsp maple syrup

4 soft flour standing tortillas

100g vegan cheese, grated

Juice of 1 lime

1 avocado, stoned, peeled and sliced (or use guacamole)

Add half the oil to a pan and place over a medium heat, then add the grated potato and cook for 10 minutes. Add the garlic, onion, chillies and walnuts to the pan and stir. Season with the paprika, onion salt, BBQ sauce and maple syrup and cook over a low heat for 5 minutes.

Preheat the oven to 160°C/140°C Fan/325°F/gas 3.

Place the standing tortillas on a baking tray, and stuff them with the walnut mix until they are each about three-quarters full. Squeeze lime juice on to each and bake in the oven for 15 minutes.

Take out of the oven, add a sprinkle of vegan cheese and add a dollop of guacamole or sliced avocado to each taco, serving two per person.

TIP
You can also replace the filling with the Chilli non carne (see page 119) to mix it up!

Every roast dinner needs a centrepiece, and this hasselback squash fits the bill. Try this paired with Roasted new potatoes and garlic aioli (see page 101) or a fresh potato salad.

# Hasselback squash

SERVES 4

1 butternut squash
A drizzle of olive oil
2 tbsp garlic purée
1 tbsp fresh thyme (or use dried)
Pinch of sea salt

Preheat the oven to 180°C/160°C Fan/350°F/gas 4.

Peel the thick skin of your butternut squash using a vegetable peeler to expose the rich, deep orange colour of the flesh. Cut the squash in half and scoop out the seeds. Place wooden spatula handles on the cutting board on either side of the squash – these will be your guide to make sure you don't cut right through the squash. Now make ½cm (¼in) incisions along the squash, stopping as you reach the spatula handles.

Mix the olive oil and garlic purée in a small bowl and brush all over the squash, getting into all of the cuts. Season with thyme and salt. Bake for 40 minutes. Serve as the centrepiece of your roast dinner.

# Roast dinner ready?

Why not accompany the squash with these sides:

---

**ROAST POTATOES** — Peel and quarter 250g Maris Piper potatoes per person, add to a baking tray, drizzle with olive oil, season with salt and freshly chopped rosemary and roast in the oven at 180°C/160°C Fan/350°F/gas 4 for 40 minutes. For extra crispiness, halfway through crush them all slightly with a potato masher or the back of a fork to allow for the oil to soak deeper into the potato.

**TENDERSTEM BROCCOLI** — Why not try steaming your broccoli then adding a knob of vegan butter and a little sea salt?

**MAPLE CARROTS** — You don't need honey to glaze your carrots! Add a tablespoon of maple syrup and some olive oil and roast your carrots on a baking tray with coarse salt.

**CABBAGE** — One thing everyone needs more of is dark leafy greens, so why not chop some cabbage into strips and steam it for your roast dinner?

**GET STUFFED!** — Stuffing is a must for my roast dinners. Combine 100g (½ cup) cooked pearl barley, 60g (½ cup) chopped walnuts, 1 bunch of sage leaves, chopped, ½ teaspoon dried parsley and 100g (2 cups) soft breadcrumbs. Melt 75g vegan butter, fry 1 large finely chopped onion for 5 minutes, add in the rest of the ingredients and stir to combine. Tip into a baking dish and bake in the oven for 40 minutes at 180°C/160°C Fan/350°F/gas 4.

Basically, this is baked pumpkin, Italian-style. Butternut squash is versatile and tasty but this is perhaps the best way to use it, as it adds so much flavour to this autumnal dish.

# Zucca al forno

SERVES 4

1 butternut squash, halved, deseeded and cut into thick slices

3–4 tbsp olive oil

10g sage leaves, roughly chopped, or 3 tsp dried sage

1 tsp cracked black pepper

1 tsp grated nutmeg

1 tsp chilli flakes

Pinch of coarse salt

Handful of raisins

3 garlic cloves, lightly crushed and quartered

Preheat the oven to 200°C/180°C Fan/400°F/gas 6.

Place the squash slices in a bowl, then pour over the olive oil to coat.

Sprinkle over the sage, pepper, nutmeg, chilli flakes and salt and mix in to evenly coat the squash.

Transfer to a deep baking tray, spacing them out so they aren't on top of each other, then scatter over the raisins and garlic cloves. Cover the tray with tinfoil and bake for 25 minutes. Remove the foil, then bake for another 15 minutes.

Serve the baked squash with a fresh salad or as a side dish.

This dip is tasty and versatile, great for dipping bread in, or used as a tasty spread or in a sauce. Try it and find your favourite way.

# Sundried tomato, red pepper and garlic dip

MAKES 1 BOWL

4 garlic cloves, crushed

4 tbsp olive oil

1 tsp oregano leaves

75g (½ cup) cherry
  tomatoes

55g (1 cup) sundried
  tomatoes in oil, drained
  and chopped

1 tbsp chopped basil

1 roasted red pepper

Pinch of black pepper

Add the garlic, olive oil, oregano and cherry tomatoes to a food processor and blend to a rough sauce.

Add the sundried tomatoes and red pepper to the food processor and pulse briefly – just a few pulses will do, you want it to still be a little bit chunky.

Serve!

This is hands down my favourite dish of all time... I created it on my travels through Italy, while staying in a little town called Zevio. I was met with such kindness by the locals that I decided to dedicate this dish to them. It always goes down a treat and is packed full of veg and pulses.

# Zeviostrone

SERVES 4

Olive oil, for frying

1 large onion, finely chopped

4 garlic cloves, finely chopped

4 green chillies, finely chopped

2 carrots, finely chopped

2 celery sticks, finely chopped

3 large tomatoes, chopped

½ x 400g tin cannellini beans, rinsed and drained

½ x 400g tin borlotti beans, rinsed and drained

500ml (2 cups) vegetable stock (from a cube)

150g (1½ cups) short pasta tubes

Big bunch of spinach, roughly chopped

Handful of basil, roughly chopped

3 tbsp (¾ cup) nutritional yeast

4 tbsp Vegan pesto (see page 40)

Pinch of dried oregano

Pinch of salt and pepper

Heat the olive oil in a large pan over a low heat. Add the onion, garlic and chillies and cook for 5 minutes until the onions are softened. Add the carrots, celery and tomatoes and cook over a low heat for 5 minutes. Now into the pan go the beans and stock, stir this all together and add the pasta. Cook for 10 minutes.

Add the spinach and basil to the pan, then stir in the nutritional yeast and most of the pesto, along with the oregano, salt and pepper, then simmer for a further 5 minutes.

Serve in a deep dish with a dollop of pesto and garnished with a sprig of basil. Enjoy!

After making a raw lasagne for my first interview with the founder of UK Vegan Campout, Jordan Goodridge, I decided to mix things up and create this open lasagne dish for our second interview. This recipe has a tasty vegan Bolognese sauce with a cheesy creamy sauce poured over the top. Delicious from start to finish.

# Open lasagne

SERVES 4

*For the Bolognese sauce*
Olive oil, for frying
1 onion, finely chopped
3 garlic cloves, finely
   chopped
2 celery sticks, thinly sliced
1 carrot, sliced
225g (1 cup) vegan frozen
   soy mince
4 tbsp red wine or 3 tbsp
   cranberry juice and 1
   tbsp apple cider vinegar
3 tbsp (¾ cup) nutritional
   yeast
1 vegan vegetable stock
   cube
1 tsp dried oregano
Pinch of salt
Generous grind of black
   pepper
250ml (1 cup) passata
Bunch of basil, finely
   chopped

(continued...)

For the Bolognese sauce, heat the oil in a pan over a low heat and cook the onion and garlic for a few minutes until translucent, then add the celery. Cook for a few minutes then add the carrot to the pan along with the soy mince, and cook for a few minutes before adding the wine or alternative. Sprinkle with the nutritional yeast, crumble in the stock cube, and season with oregano, salt and pepper.

Once the mince has cooked, add the passata, 125ml (½ cup) water and the basil. Stir and cook to thicken for 10–15 minutes.

Meanwhile, make the white sauce. Add the soy cream or alternative and cheese or alternative to a small pan and cook until it thickens – the amount of time this will take varies depending on the ingredients, but keep over a low heat and stir slowly and often for about 15 minutes. Add black pepper to taste.

Cook the pasta in a pan of boiling water following the packet instructions.

Drain the pasta and divide among bowls, spoon the Bolognese sauce on top, followed by the white sauce.

Sprinkle with nutritional yeast and black pepper and serve with basil or peppery salad.

*For the white sauce*
125ml (½ cup) soy or oat
   cream (or 250ml
   (1 cup) plant-based milk
   reduced by half by
   simmering)
30g (¼ cup) grated vegan
   cheese (or 3 more tbsp
   of nutritional yeast)
Black pepper, to taste

*To serve*
Vegan pappardelle-style
   pasta
Sprinkling of nutritional
   yeast
Basil leaves or peppery
   salad

TIP
If you want to reduce the amount of soy you eat you can use 1 cup of porcini mushrooms instead of the soy mince. Increase the amount of water to 250ml (1 cup) and dissolve the stock cube in it. Soak the porcini mushrooms in this for 15 minutes before adding to the Bolognese sauce.

Not only is this dish tasty and satisfying it is also incredibly beautiful and impressive when constructed. A dish for winning hearts and minds.

# Gourmet gratin

SERVES 4

Vegan butter, for greasing
1kg new potatoes, cut into
　2mm slices
Olive oil, for frying
2 shallots, thinly sliced
2 garlic cloves, halved
Pinch of grated nutmeg
500ml (2 cups) soy or oat
　cream (or 600ml cashew
　milk thickened over a
　low heat for 20 minutes)
2 tsp Dijon mustard
100g vegan cheese
　(optional)
Salt and black pepper

*For the red pepper and*
　*butternut purée*
200g (1 cup) butternut
　squash cubes
1 red pepper, deseeded
　and roughly chopped

*To serve*
Steamed broccoli
Dijon mustard

Preheat the oven to 180°C/160°C Fan/350°F/gas 4. Grease the base of a 25 x 15cm (10 x 6in) baking tin.

Rinse the potato slices in a large bowl of water, then drain and wrap in a tea towel.

Heat the olive oil in a frying pan over a medium heat and fry the shallots and garlic for a couple of minutes until softened.

Heat the cream or milk in a pan until bubbles start to form and the cream is close to boiling point. Remove from the heat and stir in the Dijon mustard.

Layer half the potato slices in the greased tin, slightly overlapping the slices and sprinkling with a little of the cheese, if using, and salt and pepper between each layer. Halfway through, pour half the liquid over the potatoes, then finish layering the rest of the potatoes. Pour over the remaining liquid, top with more cheese and a sprinkle of nutmeg.

Cover the baking tin with tin foil and bake in the oven for 1 hour. Remove the foil and cook for another 20 minutes. Leave to rest for 5–10 minutes.

Meanwhile, make the red pepper and butternut purée. Blend all the ingredients together in a blender, then transfer to a small pan and heat for 10 minutes.

Serve the gratin with the purée on the side, along with some steamed broccoli and mustard.

Cooked during my interview with the boys from BOSH!, this is a tasty but healthy dish that really packs in the flavour. Great for a curry night in. Add more chilli if you like it hot. This is perfect alongside Thai rice.

# Thai green greens

SERVES 4

*For the Thai green sauce*
3 large green chillies, deseeded and chopped
4 garlic cloves, crushed
3 shallots, roughly chopped
5cm (2in) piece of fresh ginger, peeled and grated
Small bunch of coriander
1 lemongrass stalk, chopped
1 tbsp coriander seeds, crushed
1 tsp cumin seeds, crushed
1 tsp black peppercorns, crushed
1 tsp Himalayan salt
Small bunch of Thai basil
Grated zest and juice of 1½ limes
175ml (¾ cup) coconut milk

*For the green greens*
3 tbsp coconut oil
4 tsp light soy sauce
Handful of Tendersteam broccoli stems
Handful of green beans
Handful of mangetout
60ml (¼ cup) maple syrup

First make the Thai green sauce. Put all the ingredients into a blender, reserving a few coriander leaves to garnish. Whizz to a smooth sauce.

Now for the greens. In a pan or wok, heat the coconut oil and soy sauce over a medium heat. When the pan is hot, add in the broccoli, green beans and mangetout and lightly fry for a few minutes, then add the maple syrup. Toss the veg in the syrup before adding the sweet Thai green sauce. Coat the veg and simmer to thicken for 10 minutes.

Scatter with the remaining coriander leaves and serve.

Risotto is a real favourite of mine; it is a delicious yet simple.
Do it right and there are few meals better than this.

# Asparagus risotto

SERVES 4

2 tbsp olive oil

2 shallots, finely chopped

3 garlic cloves, very finely chopped

3 tbsp (¾ cup) nutritional yeast

400g (1¾ cups) risotto rice

150ml (generous ½ cup) vegan white wine

1 litre (4 cups) vegetable stock

150g (1 cup) frozen peas

Bunch of thin-stemmed asparagus (about 10 stems)

Salt and pepper, to taste

Handful of parsley, roughly chopped, to garnish

Heat the oil in a large, deep pan or wok over a medium heat. Fry the shallots for a few minutes until softened and lightly browned, then add the garlic and nutritional yeast.

Tip the rice into the pan and toast it for 1 minute before pouring in the wine. Let the alcohol burn off for a minute or so, then add the first ladle of vegetable stock. The trick is to keep the dish over a high heat and stir regularly until the liquid is absorbed, then add another ladle. Repeat this until the stock is all used up. Add the peas and allow to simmer for another 5 minutes.

While the risotto is simmering, add a little oil to a hot pan (a griddle pan is best) and sear the asparagus stems for a couple of minutes until tender and char-marked. Chop each stem into roughly 5 pieces, then add to the risotto and allow to stand for 5 minutes.

Seasom with salt and black pepper and serve with some parsley scattered over.

One of my go-to meals when I was younger was gnocchi and pesto – and not much has changed. I taught the world-class comedian Owen Smith how to make this dish during my visit to Los Angeles, and it went down a treat. Try the White wine and pesto gnocchi on the next page.

# Gnocchi

SERVES 4

400g King Edwards or
    Maris Piper floury
    potatoes
Pinch of sea salt
100g (scant 1 cup) plain
    flour, plus extra for
    dusting

Bring a large pan of salted water to the boil, add the potatoes – with the skins still on – and simmer for 30 minutes until tender and ready to mash. Drain, and rub off the skins using a tea towel. Leave the potatoes to steam for 10 minutes, then mash them until smooth.

Add a pinch of salt and the flour, 1 tablespoon at a time, stirring after each addition. Keep adding flour until the dough is no longer sticky to touch and retains its shape when a small piece is moulded into a ball.

Tip the dough on to a work surface lightly dusted with flour and roll into a long sausage two finger-widths wide. Slice at 2.5cm (1in) intervals and roll each chunk into a small oval then press gently to flatten slightly.

Drop the gnocchi into a pan of salted boiling water and cook for 2 minutes (the gnocchi will float to the surface when they are ready).

Scoop out the cooked gnocchi using a slotted spoon and serve immediately with Vegan pesto or Marinara sauce (see pages 40 and 75) or see the recipe on the following page.

A truly romantic meal. This dish is full of flavour but not too heavy. Make the gnocchi from scratch (see previous page) and really show off your cooking skills.

# White wine and pesto gnocchi

SERVES 2

Oil, for frying
2 shallots, thinly sliced
2 garlic cloves, thinly sliced
60ml (¼ cup) white wine
2 tbsp Vegan pesto (see page 40)
125ml (½ cup) soy cream
1 bag of spinach, roughly chopped
½ portion of homemade gnocchi (see page 141), or shop-bought, but check milk and egg free
6 Tenderstem broccoli stems, steamed
Small bunch of basil (25g)

Heat the oil in a large frying pan over a medium heat. Add the shallots and cook for a few minutes to soften before adding the garlic. Once the garlic and shallots are translucent after a few minutes, pour in the wine and cook for 30 seconds to burn off the alcohol. Stir in the pesto, soy cream and spinach, then add in the gnocchi and stir to coat. Cook for 10 minutes.

Meanwhile, steam the broccoli for 3–4 minutes until it is cooked but still has some bite.

Serve the gnocchi scattered with basil leaves and the broccoli stems laid on top.

# AT THE WEEKEND

## STREET FOOD

Spring roll burritos

Hash daddy

Mac and cheese

Mac and cheese burger

Asian veggie kebabs

Italian veggie kebabs

Asian veggie kofte

Thai curried tofu skewers

Easy escalivada

Sticky tamarind patatas

Chilli bean toastie

## STEALING THE SHOW

Spanish frittata

Vegan nduja calzone

Parmigiana calzone

Italian flag lasagne

Smoked paprika and maple syrup dough balls

Brilliant basic bread

Stuffed sag aloo bread

Like spring rolls but can't be bothered to make your own? Why not try this easy twist? Spring roll burritos are a hearty alternative filled with a tasty satay sauce.

# Spring roll burritos

SERVES 4

Drizzle of olive oil
¼ small cabbage, thinly
    sliced
1 carrot, grated
200g beansprouts
3 spring onions, thinly sliced
100g chestnut mushrooms,
    diced
2 tbsp smooth peanut
    butter
Drizzle of soy sauce
1½ tbsp garlic purée
3 tbsp golden syrup
6 tortillas
Handful of sesame seeds

Drizzle the olive oil into a wok set over a low heat, add all the vegetables and cook them for 15 minutes.

While the vegetables are cooking, mix together the peanut butter, soy sauce, garlic purée and golden syrup in a bowl and set to one side.

Warm the tortillas, one at a time, in a pan over an extremely low heat to only allow the tortilla to warm through and not crisp – the tortilla should become more flexible, reducing the risk of splitting during the rolling process.

Take one tortilla and place a spoonful of the vegetable mix into the centre, cover with a spoonful of peanut butter and garlic sauce and sprinkle with sesame seeds. To roll the burrito, fold the edge nearest to you over the filling, then press down and scrape the mixture towards you, encasing it in the centre of the burrito. Taking your little finger and thumb, press down firmly on the edges of the mixture through the burrito and trap all of the mixture inside. Now fold the two outer edges in left and right and roll the burrito away tightly.

Place the burritos in a pan over a low heat with a little oil, making sure you place the exposed flap downwards. After a few minutes, turn the burritos, making sure they are golden on both sides.

Serve immediately with the remaining sticky peanut butter and garlic sauce.

Fried potato is a real favourite of mine, and I wanted to build a dish around that delight. Don't keep this for breakfast, this is suitable for any meal of the day. There's no time like the present, so give it a go.

## Hash daddy

SERVES 2

200g potatoes (any type)
Drizzle of olive oil
1 small onion, roughly
　chopped
2 garlic cloves, finely
　chopped
100g chestnut mushrooms,
　sliced
100g tinned black beans,
　drained
2 tbsp Peppered cashew
　cheese sauce (see page
　52)
½ avocado, stoned and
　thinly sliced (optional)
Smoked paprika or chilli
　flakes, to garnish

Grate the potatoes, put them in a sieve, rinse under running water, then tip them into a clean tea towel and pat dry.

Heat the olive oil in a large frying over a low heat, then fry the onion and garlic gently for 2 minutes.

Add the potatoes and fry over a low heat for 10 minutes. Now add the mushrooms and black beans to the pan and fry for a further 10 minutes.

Divide the mixture between 2 small plates. Add a tablespoon of peppered cashew cheese and top with the avocado slices, if using, and sprinkle with smoked paprika or chilli flakes.

A real vegan classic. When you first realise you can still have mac and cheese and be vegan, you realise that life is full of wonder and possibility. Why not make extra and give the burger on page 151 a go? I promise you won't be disappointed. Try Follow Your Heart pizza shreds cheese as it melts really well.

# Mac and cheese

SERVES 4

80g vegan butter

1 large onion, finely chopped

3 garlic cloves, finely chopped

2 tbsp plain flour

75g (1¼ cups) nutritional yeast

1 tsp dried thyme

500ml (2 cups) cashew milk

150g (1½ cups) dried macaroni

80g vegan cheese

Salt and pepper, to taste

Melt the vegan butter in a pan over a low heat, then add the onion and cook for a few minutes.

Add the garlic and cook for a few minutes, then add the flour, nutritional yeast and thyme, lower the heat right down and stir. Pour the milk in and stir on a low heat for roughly 20 minutes to thicken.

Meanwhile, cook the macaroni in a pan of boiling water for 15 minutes. Drain and tip into the cream, stir, then simmer over a low heat for 5-10 minutes.

Add the vegan cheese and stir until melted.

Season to taste , then serve while hot.

Yes, you read that right, mac and cheese burger. This was one of the first meals I ever posted on Instagram and the really great feedback I got might be the reason I still make delicious vegan food today. There are few dishes more decadent than this. Not for every day, but amazing for special occasions.

# Mac and cheese burger

SERVES 2

150g Mac and cheese (see page 149) chilled (as much as you can pack into two 8cm (3in) cutters)
2 tbsp plain flour
75ml (⅓ cup) plant-based milk
5 tbsp panko breadcrumbs
500ml (2 cups) vegetable oil

*To serve*
2 buns, cut in half
Vegan mayo
Tomato, BBQ or sriracha sauce
Rainbow slaw (see page 107)
Avocado or tomato slices
Onion slices
Gherkins
Lettuce leaves

Pack the mac and cheese into 2 cookie cutters, place on a plate and leave in the fridge to set for 2 hours.

Put the flour, milk and breadcrumbs into three separate plates. Press the pasta patty in the flour on both sides, then brush with the milk and press the patty into the breadcrumbs to coat all over.

Fill a small pan with the vegetable oil and place over a medium heat (to check the oil is hot enough sprinkle in a few breadcrumbs – they should fizz and bubble).

Lower the patties carefully into the hot oil, one at a time, and fry for 3–5 minutes until golden brown all over. Remove with a slotted spatula and transfer to a plate lined with kitchen paper.

Spread your preferred sauce or mayo over the base bun, then add the mac and cheese patty and top with anything you like – slaw, avocado or tomato slices, onions, gherkins, lettuce, etc.

One of the common misconceptions about vegans is that they don't barbecue food. That is simply not the case, so to prove it, try these Asian veggie kebabs for an awesome addition to your barbecue buffet. Photographed here with Italian veggie kebabs (see overleaf).

# Asian veggie kebabs

MAKES 6 KEBABS

4 tbsp hoisin sauce

2 tbsp soy sauce

3 tbsp vegetable oil

1 x 400g block of firm tofu, cut into 1cm (½in) cubes

4 peaches, each sliced into 6 segments

200g mushrooms, halved

2 large onions, each cut into 12 chunks

2 heads of broccoli, cut into small florets

Preheat the oven to 180°C/160°C Fan/350°F/gas 4.

Mix the hoisin and soy sauces and vegetable oil in a small bowl and set aside.

Now assemble the skewers by alternating the ingredients evenly on to 6 skewers. Brush them with the hoisin mix, then place on a plate or baking tray, cover and place in the fridge for at least a few hours, to help the kebabs absorb the hoisin flavour.

Cook in the oven for 20 minutes, then finish on a hot barbecue for added flavour.

These Italian veggie kebabs show how simple and delicious ingredients always work well together. Skewer up some colourful kebabs and bring them out when it's party time. See photo on previous page.

## Italian veggie kebabs

MAKES 6 KEBABS

75ml (⅓ cup) olive oil

75ml (⅓ cup) balsamic vinegar (preferably a glaze type, which is thicker)

500g cherry tomatoes

2 large courgettes, cut into discs

2 aubergines, cut into discs

400g pitted olives

12 large garlic cloves, peeled

12 artichoke slices

1 tsp dried basil

1 tsp dried oregano

½ tsp salt

Preheat the oven to 180°C/160°C Fan/350°F/gas 4.

Mix together the olive oil and balsamic vinegar in a bowl and set aside.

Assemble the kebabs by alternating the ingredients evenly on to 6 skewers. Brush the skewers with the balsamic and olive oil glaze, then sprinkle with the basil, oregano and salt.

Cook in the oven for 20 minutes, then finish on a hot barbecue for added flavour.

Koftes are a must at a barbecue. These Asian versions are delicious and contain tons of veggies.

# Asian veggie kofte

SERVES 4

1 tsp five-spice powder

½ tsp ground ginger

2 tbsp garlic purée or 3 finely chopped garlic cloves

Big bunch of coriander

3 tbsp hoisin sauce

1 courgette, roughly chopped

1 x 400g tin chickpeas, rinsed and drained

2 medium carrots, grated

80g fine breadcrumbs

2 tbsp flour

Olive oil, for frying

Put the five-spice, ginger, garlic, coriander and hoisin sauce into a food processor or blender along with the courgette and blitz roughly. Tip out into a large bowl, add the drained chickpeas and use a potato masher to mash until combined but still lumpy (less is more). Add the grated carrots, breadcrumbs and flour, then mix until all combined.

Divide the mixture into 8 and shape into kofte (or you can make these into 4 patties), place on a plate, cover with cling film and put in the fridge for 30 minutes to firm up.

Heat the oil in a frying pan over a medium heat and cook the koftes on each side for a couple of minutes until browned, turning them carefully so they don't break up.

Street food

This is an adaptation of one of the best meals I ate in San Diego. My friend Janette and I went out for a meal in the city after crossing the border from Mexico, and this dish made the trip complete; I have recreated my own version.

# Thai curried tofu skewers

SERVES 2

*For the kebab skewers*
1 x 400g block of firm tofu, cut into 2.5cm (1in) cubes
Drizzle of coconut milk
Drizzle of maple syrup
Handful of coriander, chopped

*For the green curry*
1 shallot, roughly chopped
1 large green chilli, deseeded and chopped
1 garlic clove
2.5cm (1in) piece of fresh ginger
Small bunch of coriander
Small bunch of Thai basil
1 lemongrass stalk, chopped
Juice of ½ lime
½ tsp ground cumin

*For the red curry*
1 shallot, roughly chopped
1 large red chilli, deseeded and chopped
1 garlic clove
5 cherry tomatoes
75ml (⅓ cup) maple syrup
60ml (¼ cup) coconut milk

First make the curry sauces. Put all the ingredients for the green curry sauce in a blender and blitz to a smooth paste. Transfer to a bowl. Clean out the blender and repeat with the red curry sauce ingredients. Put the bowl of red curry sauce in the fridge.

Push 5 pieces of tofu on to each of 6 skewers and set in a shallow dish or deep plate. Pour over the green curry sauce to cover the tofu. Cover and put in the fridge for at least a few hours, or preferably overnight, to allow the tofu to absorb the flavours.

Preheat the oven to 200°C/180°C Fan/400°F/gas 6. Transfer the skewers to a baking sheet and bake for 20 minutes, turning them halfway through the cooking time.

Meanwhile, heat the red curry sauce in a small pan, stirring occasionally. Plate up 3 skewers per person and drizzle each skewer with 1 tablespoon red curry sauce. Drizzle with a little coconut milk then a little maple syrup and garnish with chopped coriander.

Escalivada is a go-to dish for tapas-loving vegans. A traditional Spanish dish, it is full of flavour and simple to recreate.

# Easy escalivada

2 small aubergines

2 red peppers

2 tomatoes

2 large spring onions

70ml (generous ¼ cup) extra virgin olive oil, plus extra for brushing

2 garlic cloves, thinly sliced

Salt, to taste

Handful of parsley, roughly chopped

Preheat the oven to 240°C/220°C Fan/450°F/gas 8.

Brush all of the vegetables with olive oil, then arrange them, whole, on a baking tray or in a roasting tin and roast for 30 minutes, turning them halfway through the cooking time.

Remove the vegetables from the oven, cover with tinfoil and allow them to cool.

Once cool, peel the aubergines, peppers and tomatoes, and remove the outer layer of the onions.

Tear the peppers in half, remove the seeds, then slice into 1cm (½in) strips. Do the same with the tomatoes. Cut the onions into rings and add to the bowl along with the garlic. Add the olive oil, season with salt and toss to mix and coat all the vegetables.

Serve at room temperature, garnished with the parsley.

Street food

These sticky tamarind patatas are potatoes which are cubed just like patatas bravas, but then coated in a sweet, sticky tamarind sauce that will keep you coming back for more. Depending on your tolerance of heat, you could serve these scattered with some slices of fresh green chilli.

## Sticky tamarind patatas

SERVES 2–4 AS A SIDE

2 large potatoes (Red Rooster are best), cut into 2.5cm (1in) cubes
2 tbsp oil (coconut is best)
2 tbsp treacle
1 tsp tamarind paste
½ tsp salt
Sprigs of tarragon, chopped

Preheat the oven to 180°C/160°C Fan/350°F/gas 4.

Drop the potatoes into a bowl of cold water to remove some of the starch and help them crisp up. Drain, tip into a large bowl, pour over the oil and mix to coat.

Place the potatoes on a baking tray, cover with tin foil and bake in the oven for 25 minutes.

Meanwhile, combine the treacle and tamarind paste in a small bowl.

Remove the potatoes from the oven, tip into a bowl, add the treacle and tamarind mix and coat well before returning to the baking tray and seasoning with salt. Bake for a further 15 minutes.

Serve hot with the chopped tarragon scattered over.

This is the ultimate in comfort food cooking! Warm, melting toastie goodness for a chilly day is a must. Try Follow Your Heart pizza shreds or Sainsbury's Freefrom vegan cheese.

## Chilli bean toastie

SERVES 1

White bloomer loaf
60g (½ cup) vegan cheese
3 tbsp Chilli non carne (see page 119), or use tinned beans in chilli sauce

Using a sharp bread knife, cut into the loaf to make a 2cm (¾in) slice, but stop at the crusty base – just as you would when cutting a bun or roll, do not cut all the way through. On the next slice, cut all the way through so you have the two slices connected by the bottom crust – almost like a pitta.

Fill the sandwich with half the cheese then scoop in the chilli (if you are using tinned beans, warm them on the hob first to thicken the sauce), followed by the remaining cheese.

To toast, use a flat-plate panini maker or grilling machine if you have one, or just bake on a baking tray in a preheated oven (15 minutes at 150°C/130°C Fan/300°F/gas 2).

Enjoy on its own or with a warming Wholesome tomato soup (see page 49) on those drizzly cold days!

Once I had perfected the vegan omelette, a frittata was an immediate must. This is one of my favourite dishes – make this and serve it to anyone and you will hear nothing but praise.

# Spanish frittata

SERVES 4

*For the omelette mix*
1 x 400g block of firm tofu
4 tbsp nutritional yeast
120g (1 cup) gram
   (chickpea) flour
3 tsp cornflour
½ tsp turmeric
Pinch of smoked paprika
½ tsp salt
180ml (¾ cup) aquafaba
   (juice from a tin of
   chickpeas)
1 tbsp olive oil

*For the frittata filling*
50ml (scant ¼ cup) extra
   virgin olive oil
300g new potatoes, cut
   into thin slices
1 white onion, sliced
1 red pepper, deseeded
   and cut into thin strips
Handful of spinach, roughly
   chopped
100g vegan cheese, grated
   (optional)
Pinch of salt and pepper
3 tbsp chopped flat-leaf
   parsley, to garnish

Put all the omelette ingredients into a food processor or blender and whizz until the mixture is smooth and there are no lumps.

Heat the olive oil in a large pan over a medium heat and fry the potatoes for 15 minutes, stirring occasionally. Lower the heat, add the onion and red pepper and cook for 10 minutes. Add the spinach and then pour in the batter mixture to completely cover the vegetables. Turn the heat down to the lowest setting and cook for 10 minutes.

Transfer the pan to the grill and cook under a very low heat – if you are adding vegan cheese do it now – for 10 minutes.

Season with a pinch of salt and pepper, garnish with the parsley and serve hot.

A calzone is basically a folded pizza filled with whatever delights you please. Nduja is a spicy sausage and classic pizza topping. Here I have given a great vegan version that will really satisfy your taste buds.

# Vegan nduja calzone

SERVES 2

1 portion of pizza dough (see page 115)
70ml (¼ cup) sieved passata
4 vegan sausages (Linda McCartney or similar)
2 red chillies, finely chopped
1 shallot, thinly sliced
1 bag of spinach, finely chopped
80g vegan cheese (optional)
½ tsp dried oregano or a few sprigs of oregano, roughly chopped
Marinara sauce (see page 75), to serve

Preheat the oven to 180°C/160°C Fan/350°F/gas 4.

Stretch the dough out into a large circle (see page 115).

Transfer the dough to a baking sheet and spread the passata thinly over half of the circle, keeping it 1cm (½in) from the edge.

Crumble over the sausages, the chopped chillies, shallot, spinach, cheese, if using, and oregano.

Fold over the side of the pizza base without the filling and lightly press down on the edges to seal. Bake for 12 minutes until golden.

Serve topped with marinara sauce.

TIP
To remove some of the flour and seal the calzone completely, use a little passata on your finger to wet the edges of the dough when sealing.

Stealing the show

Based on my favourite pizza from my favourite pizza spot, PickyWops, a pizzeria in Fulham and Peckham, the full moon parmigiana is a winner because of its amazing flavour combination.

# Parmigiana calzone

SERVES 2

1 x portion of pizza dough (see page 115)

70ml (¼ cup) sieved passata

1 tbsp olive oil

1 large aubergine, thinly sliced

2 shallots, thinly sliced

2 garlic cloves, finely chopped

4 tbsp nutritional yeast

Small bunch of basil, torn

1 tbsp Vegan pesto (see page 40)

80g vegan cheese, grated (optional)

Marinara sauce (see page 75), to serve

Preheat the oven to 180°C/160°C Fan/350°F/gas 4.

Stretch the dough out into a large circle (see page 115).

Transfer the dough to a baking sheet and spread the passata thinly over half of the circle, keeping it 1cm (½in) from the edge.

Heat the olive oil in a large pan over a low heat and fry the aubergine slices with the shallots and garlic for 15 minutes. Sprinkle with the nutritional yeast and cook for another 10 minutes.

Scatter the aubergine mix over the passata and top with torn basil leaves, pesto and vegan cheese, if using. Fold over the side of the pizza base without the filling and lightly press down on the edges to seal. Bake for 12 minutes until golden.

Serve topped with marinara sauce.

I first created this dish for my appearance on the ITV2 show *The Big Audition*; I won the competition, so I got the job as recipe creator. It was a proud moment when a traditional Italian chef tucked into my lasagne and announced it as good as any he had ever tasted. See photo overleaf.

# Italian flag lasagne

SERVES 6-8

150g (1 cup) macadamia nuts
27 lasagne sheets, plain or spinach, or use half and half
Olive oil, for frying
2 courgettes, very thinly sliced
5 tbsp Vegan pesto (see page 40), plus extra to serve
4 tbsp nutritional yeast
2 yellow peppers, deseeded and sliced
250ml (1 cup) soy cream or oat milk
600g passata
1 tbsp garlic purée
2 tbsp tomato and basil purée
80g vegan cheese, grated (optional)
Basil sprigs, to garnish

Preheat the oven to 180°C/160°C Fan/350°F/gas 4.

Soak the macadamia nuts in a small bowl of water for at least 1 hour. Soak the pasta sheets in warm water until ready to use.

Heat a generous helping of olive oil in a pan over a very low heat and cook the courgette slices until they begin to wilt and soften. Take off the heat, stir in the pesto and set aside.

Drain the nuts and add with the nutritional yeast, yellow peppers and soy cream or oat milk to a blender and blend into a smooth sauce.

Add the passata and tomato and garlic purées to a bowl and stir together.

Drain the pasta sheets. In a 20cm (8in) square baking dish, spread 2 tablespoons of red sauce over the base of the dish, then add a layer of plain pasta sheets – you will probably need 3 per layer, overlapping. Top these with a layer of red sauce, then cover with the green sheets. Cover with the white sauce, then a layer of white sheets. Spread these with pesto and cover with the courgette slices and green pasta sheets. Repeat this process until you have 6-9 layers. Finish with a layer of red sauce and then white sauce on top.

Cover the dish with tinfoil and bake in the oven for 40 minutes, until the pasta is cooked through and tender.

After 40 minutes, if you like, you can add a layer of grated cheese, then remove the tinfoil and bake for a further 10 minutes.

Remove from the oven and allow the lasgne to rest for 5 minutes, then slice up carefully, trying to maintain the layers as much as possible. Garnish with a teaspoon of pesto and sprig of basil.

TIP
To pre-cook the lasagne sheets and gain the best results; lay the sheets out in 2 large baking trays and cover with boiling water. Try not to overlap them as this will cause them to stick and pulling them apart may tear them.

Stealing the show

With smoked paprika and maple syrup glaze these tear and share dough balls are great to serve to friends and family. Serve with olive oil, balsamic vinegar and your favourite dips.

# Smoked paprika and maple syrup dough balls

SERVES 2

500g (4 cups) plain flour, plus extra for dusting
1 tsp onion salt
7g dried fast-action yeast
1 tbsp sugar
4 tbsp maple syrup
2 tbsp olive oil, plus extra for greasing
2 tbsp smoked paprika

Put the flour in a mixing bowl and mix in the onion salt. In a measuring jug, stir together 300ml (scant 1¼ cups) water, the yeast and sugar. Make a well in the centre of the flour and add in all the liquid, then stir together using a spatula. Add half the maple syrup and continue to mix.

Dust a work surface with flour and tip the dough on to it. Begin to knead the dough by taking the palm of your left hand and using it to secure the dough in place, then pushing the dough away with your right hand, stretching it and folding the dough back on itself, turning and repeating this process 20–30 times.

Grease a clean bowl with olive oil, add the dough and cover with cling film or a wet tea towel and leave to prove for 1 hour, or until the dough has doubled in size.

Preheat the oven to 180°C/160°C Fan/350°F/gas 4. Tip the dough out onto a surface dusted with flour, roll into golf-ball-sized balls. Starting with one ball in the centre of a baking tray, keep adding the balls on the outer edges, just touching, until you have a large loaf constructed of dough balls.

In a small bowl, mix together the olive oil and remaining maple syrup, and brush this over the dough balls. Sprinkle with smoked paprika and bake in the oven for 25 minutes. Remove from the oven and leave to cool slightly before eating.

Knowing how to make your own bread is an important skill, as some breads sold in supermarkets are glazed with milk or eggs. It is also very satisfying and, when mastered, opens the door to making your own stuffed breads, tear and share breads and dough ball creations.

# Brilliant basic bread

MAKES 1 LOAF

500g (4 cups) very strong white bread flour, plus extra for dusting
1 tsp salt
7g dried fast-action yeast
1 tsp sugar

Put the flour in a large mixing bowl and mix in the salt. In a measuring jug, stir together 300ml (scant 1¼ cups) water, the yeast and sugar. Make a well in the centre of the flour and add in all the liquid, then stir together using a spatula until a soft dough starts to form.

Dust a work surface with flour and tip the dough on to it. Begin to knead the dough by taking the palm of your left hand and using it to secure the dough in place, then pushing the dough away with your right hand, stretching it and folding the dough back on itself, turning and repeating this process 20–30 times.

Dust a large bowl with flour, place the dough inside and cover with a damp tea towel or cling film. Leave to prove in a warm place for about 1 hour, or until the dough has doubled in size.

Preheat the oven to 210°C/190°C Fan/400°F/gas 6. Put the dough in a lined bread tin or on the centre of a lined baking tray if you want a round loaf.

Bake for 30–40 minutes, checking after 30 minutes to see if the bread is firm and golden brown. The bread should sound hollow when the bottom is tapped. If not, pop it back in the oven for a few minutes.

Turn out of the tin and allow to cool on a wire rack for at least 30 minutes before slicing.

Using leftover sag aloo to stuff some bread was one of the best decisions I ever made. Tasty soft bread streaked with potato and spinach curry is a magnificent sight and tastes even better than it looks!

# Stuffed sag aloo bread

SERVES 4–8

8 tbsp Sag aloo (see page 98)

1 x 500g portion of Brilliant basic bread dough (see page 169)

Plant-based milk, for glazing

1 tsp cumin seeds

Chopped coriander, to garnish

Preheat the oven to 210°C/190°C Fan/400°F/gas 6.

Press flat the proved dough to a 1–2cm (½–¾in) thickness. Spoon the sag aloo into the centre and wrap it up like a parcel, being sure to seal in the curry with no leaks. Once you have sealed it, turn it over so that the folds are underneath and the top is smooth. Place on a baking tray or lined bread tin, and brush the top with a little plant-based milk. Scatter the cumin seeds over the top, and bake for 30–40 minutes.

Serve warm sprinkled with coriander.

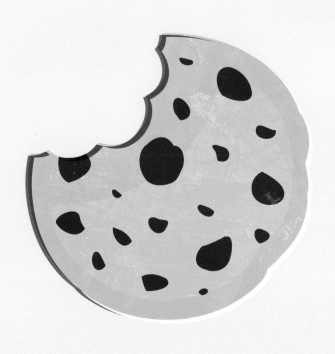

# 03

# What Vegans Eat

# For Treats

Dessert doesn't need to be complicated, and done right this incredibly simple dessert is a real winner, especially when you are cooking for a special person in your life.

# Griddled peaches with candied walnuts and ice cream

SERVES 2

3 tbsp walnut halves
60ml (¼ cup) maple syrup
Pinch of coarse sea salt
2 firm peaches, each sliced
   into 8
2 scoops of vegan ice
   cream (vanilla is best)
Soy cream (optional),
   to serve

Heat a small pan over a low heat and toast the walnut halves for a couple of minutes until lightly coloured and fragrant. Pour in the maple syrup and heat until thick and sticky, stirring to coat the nuts. Sprinkle over a small pinch of coarse salt.

Warm a large pan or griddle pan (a griddle works best because it gives beautiful charred lines on the peach), then add the peach slices. Don't touch or move them for 2 minutes, then turn them over and cook for 2 more minutes.

Transfer the peach slices to serving plates, add a scoop of ice cream to each and sprinkle with the candied walnuts. If you like, drizzle over some soy cream to serve.

Rice pudding reminds me of home. It is such a tasty, warming dish that comforts me in a way that few foods do. This banana coconut milk rice pudding is rich, creamy and perfectly balanced with sweetness.

# Banana coconut milk rice pudding

SERVES 4

135g (1 cup) pudding rice
1 x 400ml tin full-fat
    coconut milk, plus extra
    to serve
200ml (⅘ cups) cashew
    milk
120ml (½ cup) maple syrup,
    plus extra to serve
2 tsp vanilla extract
½ tsp grated nutmeg
    (optional), plus extra
    to serve
2 bananas, mashed

Put the rice into a large pan, then add all the other ingredients, except for the mashed banana. Cook gently for about 40 minutes, stirring regularly.

Stir in the mashed bananas and heat through for a minute, then remove from the heat and leave the pan to sit for 10 minutes with the lid on.

Serve sprinkled with nutmeg, if you like, and a drizzle of maple syrup and coconut milk.

Treats

I love a black forest gateau and I love milkshakes, so you
do the maths!

# Black Forest shake

SERVES 1

225g (1 cup) frozen pitted
   cherries, plus one to
   serve
60ml (¼ cup) soy milk
2 tbsp vegan chocolate
   spread
75g (½ cup) vegan vanilla
   ice cream
Coconut or soy cream,
   to top

In a blender, blitz together the cherries, milk, chocolate
spread and ice cream. Pour into a glass and add the
coconut cream top and a cherry to decorate.

As a child one of my favourite treats was banana in syrup from the takeaway. This is my twist on that nostalgic dish, but you can omit the peanut butter if classic is what you are craving.

## Peanut butter bananas

SERVES 2

2 ripe bananas, peeled
1 tbsp peanut butter
1 tbsp poppy seeds
60g (½ cup) plain flour
¼ tsp bicarbonate of soda
¼ tsp baking powder
Pinch of salt
¼ tbsp apple cider vinegar
125ml (½ cup) carbonated
   water
2 tbsp vegetable oil
Drizzle of syrup or melted
   vegan dark chocolate,
   to serve

Put the bananas on a plate and spread with the peanut butter.

Mix together the dry ingredients in a bowl, then combine the wet ingredients and pour into the flour to make a smooth batter.

Heat the vegetable oil in a small frying pan. Dip the bananas into the batter mixture and gently place in the hot oil and cook until golden brown, then turn and cook on the other side.

Remove the bananas from the pan carefully using a slotted spatula, and transfer to a plate lined with kitchen paper.

Serve the bananas with a drizzle of syrup or melted dark chocolate.

The sweet, tangy flavour of peaches makes them perfect for a crumble. An incredibly simple dessert with minimal effort.

# Peach crumble

SERVES 6

3 ripe peaches

120g (½ cup) self-raising flour

60g (generous ½ cup) rolled oats

90g vegan butter

90g (scant 1 cup) soft brown sugar

Preheat the oven to 180°C/160°C Fan/350°F/gas 4.

Cut each peach in half and remove the stones, then slice each peach into 12 (or even thinner if you prefer). Place the peach slices in an even layer in a 22cm (8½in) baking dish.

Place all the other ingredients into a large bowl and use your fingers to work everything together into a crumbly mix but don't overdo it – you don't want it to get too warm. If the mixture feels too wet, try adding some more dry ingredients.

Spread the crumble mix over the peaches evenly and bake in the oven for 35 minutes.

Serve with vegan cream, ice cream or custard.

My favourite cookie flavour but as a brownie. White chocolate chip macadamia nut blondies are a sweet treat, especially when they are still warm and just out of the oven.

# White choc chip macadamia nut blondies

SERVES 12

45g (½ cup) oat flour (oats blended to a fine powder)

60g (⅓ cup) plain flour

80g (⅓ cup) sugar

½ tsp ground cinnamon

½ tsp baking powder

370ml (1½ cups) almond milk

1 tbsp vanilla extract

200g (¾ cup) almond butter (or use peanut butter)

150g vegan white chocolate (or any vegan chocolate works), roughly chopped

100g macadamia nuts, roughly chopped

Pinch of salt

Preheat the oven to 180°C/160°C Fan/350°F/gas 4. Line a 25cm (10in) square baking tin with baking parchment.

Combine the flours, sugar, cinnamon and baking powder in a mixing bowl. Mix the milk, vanilla and nut butter together in a measuring jug until you have a smooth liquid consistency. Pour the liquid into the dry mix and stir until everything is well combined.

Stir the chocolate and macadamia nuts into the batter, then pour everything into the tin, smoothing the top of the batter. Bake in the oven for 25 minutes.

Remove the blondies from the oven and allow to cool for 30 minutes before cutting into 12 equal pieces.

Enjoy!

Oreos are one of those accidentally vegan foods that work well in so many desserts. This Oreo chocolate mousse in a jar is a simple but decadent delight. Find a jar the perfect size so that you can top the mousse with an Oreo lid for extra points.

# Oreo chocolate mousse

SERVES 4

65g (½ cup) unsweetened cocoa powder, plus 1 tbsp
175g vegan dark chocolate, broken into chunks
Pinch of sea salt
1 x 400ml tin full-fat coconut milk (oil divided, see Tip)
3 tsp vanilla extract
10 pitted Medjool dates
1–2 tbsp peanut butter (optional)
12 Oreos

In a small saucepan, combine the cocoa powder, chocolate, salt and half of the coconut milk and warm the mixture over a low heat, whisking gently to combine and melt the chocolate. Then add the remaining coconut milk and whisk until fully combined. Take off the heat and stir in the vanilla.

Transfer to a high-speed blender and add the dates, then blend until smooth. You could add a couple of tablespoons of peanut butter to mix up the flavour if you like.

Take your first jar (wide enough to fit an Oreo in) and drop 2 Oreos in on top of each other – not flat but standing on end so they fill the jar. Then pour in the mixture until it comes to within 5mm (¼in) of the top of the jar and top with a flat Oreo. Repeat for the other 3 jars. Refrigerate for at least 5 hours until set.

TIP
To divide coconut milk, leave the can in the fridge overnight to separate the oil from the milk so when you open the tin you can separate the two.

Treats

Mango lassi is a classic Indian drink that is really easy to recreate. It's great paired with a spicy curry, as the cooling coconut yoghurt will help when the spice hits. It's easiest to use frozen rather than fresh mango here as it's less preparation and you won't need any additional ice to chill the drink.

## Mango lassi

SERVES 2

330g (2 cups) frozen or
  fresh mango chunks
600ml (2 cups) vegan plain
  yoghurt
¼ tsp ground cardamom

*Optional extras*
2 tbsp lime juice
Splash of coconut milk
Ice cubes

Add the mango to a blender with the vegan yoghurt and cardamom and blitz together until smooth.

Taste, then add more cardamom if you like, plus the lime juice/coconut milk/ice cubes, if using.

Pour into glasses and drink immediately.

Treats

If you want a different type of lassi, why not give strawberry a go? If you're looking to mix things up further, you could try blending up kiwi fruit, or go half and half with strawberry.

# Strawberry lassi

SERVES 2

300g (2 cups) fresh or
  frozen strawberries
600ml (2 cups) vegan plain
  yoghurt

*Optional extras*
Splash of coconut milk
Ice cubes

Add all ingredients to a blender and blitz until smooth. Add a splash of coconut milk or some ice cubes, if you like.

Pour into glasses and drink immediately.

I was always told that carrot cake was an old wartime recipe that made the most of carrots and helped to bulk out a sweet treat when rations were slim. I absolutely love carrot cake, and this vegan version is a moist, beautiful treat that is great with a cup of tea.

# Carrot cake

SERVES 8

270g (2¼ cups) flour
3 tsp baking powder
1 tsp bicarbonate of soda
1½ tsp grated nutmeg
2 tsp ground cinnamon
Pinch of salt
120g (½ cup) granulated sugar
250ml (1 cup) plant-based milk
125g (½ cup) apple sauce
2 tsp vanilla extract
125ml (½ cup) melted coconut oil
100g (2 cups) grated carrot
200g vegan soft cheese
400g (4 cups) icing sugar
Coloured icing or crushed walnuts, to decorate

Preheat the oven to 180°C/160°C Fan/350°F/gas 4. Grease a deep 25cm (10in) loose-bottomed cake tin.

In a large bowl, mix together the flour, baking powder, bicarbonate of soda, nutmeg, cinnamon, salt and sugar.

In a measuring jug, whisk together the milk, apple sauce, vanilla and melted coconut oil. Pour the wet ingredients into the dry and mix them together with a spatula, then stir in the grated carrots.

Scrape the mixture into the cake tin. Bake in the oven for 35 minutes.

Take the cake out of the oven and allow to cool for 1 hour in the tin. Remove from the tin and leave to cool for another hour.

Meanwhile, in a large bowl, beat the vegan cheese and icing sugar together until stiff and completely combined. Place the cake on a circular plinth – preferably one that you are able to spin – and, using a spatula, spread the icing evenly over the cake, starting at the top. Decorate using coloured icing or crushed walnuts.

Add chocolate chips to a classic banana loaf and this is what you get. This is a firm favourite of mine and makes a lovely treat or snack. See photo overleaf, and pages 190 and 191 for some ideas of what else to try with banana bread.

# Chocolate chip banana bread

SERVES 8

60ml (¼ cup) vegetable oil, plus extra for greasing

240g (2 cups) plain flour, plus extra for dusting

3 medium ripe bananas, plus 1 extra, sliced lengthways

215g (½ cup) soft light brown sugar

2 tsp vanilla extract

60ml (¼ cup) plant-based milk

1 tsp bicarbonate of soda

½ tsp salt

½ tsp ground cinnamon

90g (½ cup) vegan dark chocolate chips

Preheat the oven to 180°C/160°C Fan/350°F/gas 4. Grease a 900g (2lb) loaf tin with oil, then dust it with flour, tapping out the excess.

Mush the bananas in a bowl into a lumpy mash, then add the brown sugar, oil, vanilla and plant-based milk and mix together. Sift over the flour, bicarbonate of soda, salt and cinnamon and use a wooden spoon to stir everything together well. Stir in the chocolate chips.

Transfer the batter to the loaf tin and top with the banana slices. Bake for about 40 minutes, then cover with tinfoil and bake for 10–15 minutes longer, or until a sharp knife inserted into the centre comes out with just a couple of crumbs. Leave the tin on a wire rack to cool for a few minutes, then when cooler, tip out of the tin and leave to cool completely.

Treats

Just as it says in the title, this dessert is as decadent as it gets –
chocolate chips, banana and custard, all in a baked dessert. It's my
take on a classic English pud. (See photo on previous page.)

# Decadent choc chip banana bread and butter pudding

SERVES 6

25g vegan butter, plus
extra for greasing
8 thin slices Chocolate
chip banana bread (see
page 187)
100ml (scant ½ cup)
cashew milk or rice milk
300ml vegan custard
2 tsp granulated sugar
½ tsp grated nutmeg

Grease a 13cm (5in) pie dish with vegan butter.

Spread each slice of banana bread on one side with
butter, then cut into triangles. Arrange a layer of
bread, buttered-side up, in the bottom of the dish,
and repeat to use all the slices.

Gently warm the milk and custard in a pan over a low
heat to scalding point, but don't let it boil. Add three-
quarters of the sugar and lightly whisk to combine.
Pour the custard over the bread layers and sprinkle
with nutmeg and the remaining sugar, then leave to
stand for 30 minutes.

Preheat the oven to 180°C/160°C Fan/350°F/gas 4.

Bake in the oven for 30–40 minutes, or until the
custard has set and the top is golden brown.

Treats

French toast is a real favourite of mine. So if you manage to save some banana bread, make this French toast with it for some crispy, sweet goodness.

# Banana bread French toast

SERVES 2

1 tbsp chia seeds

2 tbsp flaxseeds

½ tsp ground cinnamon

2 tbsp apple sauce

60ml (¼ cup) maple syrup, plus extra to serve

250ml (1 cup) plant-based milk

1 tsp vanilla extract

4 slices Chocolate chip banana bread (see page 187)

Oil, for frying

Fruit, to serve

Icing sugar, to serve (optional)

Blend the chia seeds, flaxseeds and cinnamon in a blender to create a fine meal. Add the apple sauce, maple syrup, plant milk and vanilla extract and blend again to combine.

Pour the mixture into a deep plate, then add the slices of banana bread and press down, turning to soak both sides.

Heat a little oil in a frying pan over a medium heat, then add the bread slices, one or two at a time, for a couple of minutes on each side until golden brown.

Serve immediately, decorated with fruit and a drizzle of maple syrup or a little dusting of icing sugar.

Dark chocolate and cherry are a delicious flavour combination and this rich dessert showcases that nicely. With such a rich and tasty tart, slices will go quickly.

# Chocolate and cherry tart

SERVES 8

*For the crust*
100g vegan margarine
300g vegan digestive
  biscuits (use Biscoff for
  best results), crushed to
  fine crumbs

*For the filling*
200g vegan dark
  chocolate, broken into
  chunks
125ml (½ cup) melted
  coconut oil
½ x 400ml tin coconut milk
1 tsp vanilla extract
250g (generous cup)
  frozen pitted cherries
1 tbsp cocoa powder, for
  dusting

Melt the margarine in a pan on a very low heat, then add the crushed biscuits and stir to combine. Use a little extra margarine to grease a 23cm (9in) tart tin and start to press the biscuit margarine mix into the tin. Press it down firmly, ensuring that you cover the tin evenly, then pop it in the fridge.

Combine the dark chocolate, coconut oil, coconut milk and vanilla extract in a pan over a low heat and cook, stirring occasionally. Once all of the chocolate has melted, pour it onto the biscuit base.

Place the cherries in the mixture, arranging them evenly over the surface of the tart, adding them until the mixture has risen level to the tin edge.

Now leave the mixture to cool in the fridge for at least 3 hours before trimming the edges. Remove the tart from the tin and dust with cocoa powder before cutting into slices.

My mum has always made the best cakes, and lemon drizzle is one that I will always associate with home. This is my blueberry lemon drizzle – inspired by her classic baking but with my own twist. Whenever baking with vinegar and bicarbonate of soda, make sure you get the cake batter into the oven quickly.

## Blueberry and lemon drizzle cake

SERVES 8

Oil spray
250g (2 cups) plain flour, plus extra for dusting
360ml (1½ cups) soy milk or oat milk
2 tsp white or apple cider vinegar
160ml (⅔ cup) melted coconut oil
125ml (½ cup) Earl Grey or breakfast tea
2 tsp vanilla extract
250g (1 cup) unsweetened apple sauce
200g (1 cup) sugar
2 tsp bicarbonate of soda
1 tsp baking powder
¼ tsp salt
150g (1 cup) blueberries, plus extra to decorate

*For the drizzle*
125ml (½ cup) lemon juice, plus zest to decorate
100g (½ cup) caster sugar
5 tbsp icing sugar

Preheat the oven to 180°C/160°C Fan/350°F/gas 4. Lightly spray a 20cm (8in) cake tins with non-stick spray. Dust with flour, shake out the excess and set aside.

Mix the milk and vinegar in a large bowl, and leave for a few minutes to activate. Add the oil, tea, vanilla extract and apple sauce and beat until foamy.

Slowly sift the flour, sugar, bicarbonate of soda, baking powder and salt over the wet ingredients while mixing with a hand-held or standing mixer. Beat until no large lumps remain.

Pour the batter into the cake tin. Evenly scatter with the blueberries and press them down with a fork. Bake for 40 minutes until a knife inserted into the centre comes out clean. If not, return to the oven and check again after 5 minutes.

Meanwhile, prepare the drizzle. Warm the lemon juice and caster sugar in a small pan over a low heat, and stir until the sugar has dissolved. Set aside.

When the cake is ready, poke holes into the cake with a toothpick. Pour half of the drizzle mixture over the top and spread it with a knife, letting it soak in. Return the rest of the mixture to the heat, add the icing sugar and stir in until it becomes a white mixture.

Remove the cake from the tin and pour over the icing mixture evenly, letting it drip down the sides. Scatter over some lemon zest and blueberries to decorate.

Muffins are the easiest cake to make when you're looking to take a sweet treat into work or add to a buffet. So why not mix up the cake batter from the previous page and make your own muffin version? Decorate each one and put your stamp on it!

# Blueberry and lemon muffins

MAKES 12

360ml (1½ cups) soy milk or oat milk

2 tsp white or apple cider vinegar

160ml (⅔ cup) melted coconut oil

125ml (½ cup) Earl Grey or breakfast tea

2 tsp vanilla extract

250g (1 cup) unsweetened apple sauce

250g (2 cups) plain flour

200g (1 cup) sugar

2 tsp bicarbonate of soda

1 tsp baking powder

¼ tsp salt

150g (1 cup) blueberries, plus extra to decorate

*For the drizzle*

125ml (½ cup) lemon juice, plus zest to decorate

100g (½ cup) caster sugar

Preheat the oven to 180°C/160°C Fan/350°F/gas 4. Place 12 muffin cases into a 12-hole muffin tin and set aside.

Mix the milk and vinegar in a large bowl, and leave for a few minutes to activate. Add the oil, tea, vanilla extract and apple sauce and beat until foamy.

Slowly sift the flour, sugar, bicarbonate of soda, baking powder and salt over the wet ingredients while mixing with a hand-held or standing mixer. Beat until no large lumps remain.

Spoon 2 tablespoons of batter into each cupcake case and add four whole blueberries to each case, pressing them until covered by the batter. Bake for 30 minutes until a knife inserted into the centre of a muffin comes out clean.

Meanwhile, prepare the drizzle. Warm the lemon juice and caster sugar in a small pan over a low heat, and stir until the sugar has dissolved. Set aside.

Once the muffins are cool, pour over the drizzle mixture evenly. Scatter over some lemon zest and a blueberry to decorate.

Chocolate desserts that have a melty middle are a surefire way to impress your guests. Pop these on the table fresh out of the oven and serve warm with some dairy-free vanilla ice cream or soy cream.

# Little chocolate and pear puddings

SERVES 4

Oil spray
5 tbsp plain flour, plus extra for dusting
80ml (generous ⅓ cup) oat milk
1 tsp apple cider vinegar
1 tbsp coconut oil
60ml (¼ cup) coffee
1 tsp vanilla extract
1 puréed pear or 2 tbsp apple sauce
1 tbsp caster sugar
3 tsp cocoa powder
½ tsp bicarbonate of soda
½ tsp baking powder
Pinch of salt
8 squares of vegan dark chocolate

Preheat the oven to 180°C/160°C Fan/350°F/gas 4. Lightly spray four 5cm (2in) cake tins with non-stick spray. Dust with flour, shake out the excess and set aside.

Mix the oat milk and vinegar in a large bowl, and leave for a few minutes to activate. Add the coconut oil, coffee, vanilla extract and puréed pear or apple sauce and beat until foamy.

Slowly sift the flour, sugar, cocoa powder, bicarbonate of soda, baking powder and salt over the wet ingredients while mixing with a hand-held or standing mixer. If you don't have a sieve, simply combine the dry ingredients in another bowl and add to the wet mixture while beating. Beat until no large lumps remain – the mix should be creamy and pourable. Taste and adjust the sweetness as needed, adding more sugar if desired.

Divide the batter evenly between the cake tins. Drop 2 squares of chocolate into each tin and push down gently so they are covered by the batter. Bake in the oven for 20 minutes.

Serve warm with a dollop of ice cream or some soy cream.

Treats

This cookie butter mousse with a brûlée lid is a delicious original dessert. The delicate texture of the cookie butter mousse topped with a crispy sugar lid makes for a unique combination.

# Cookie butter brûlée

SERVES 4

50ml (scant ¼ cup) coconut milk
250ml (1 cup) coconut cream
1 tbsp icing sugar
2 tbsp cookie butter (Biscoff biscuit spread)
2 tbsp granulated sugar

Pour the coconut milk and cream into a bowl and sift in the icing sugar, then use an electric mixer to whisk until it is light, fluffy and thick. Stir in the cookie butter and gently mix with a spatula to combine.

Cover the mixture and chill in the fridge for at least 2 hours before using it to fill 4 ramekins, leaving a small space below the rim to allow for the sugar.

Divide the sugar among the ramekins and use the flat side of a table knife to level off the sugar.

Now, the top can be caramelised by either placing the ramekins under a grill on a high heat to melt the sugar and allow the top to crisp (this is a delicate process, so be careful not to burn the sugar and take care when removing the ramekins from the grill). Or my personal preference is to use a chef's blow-torch. Keeping a uniform distance between the torch flame and the sugar, caramelise the sugar, moving the flame around the top until all of the sugar is caramelised.

Crack into that lid and enjoy!

My favourite ice cream flavour paired with amaretto liqueur is a must-try. If you don't want the alcohol, replace it with almond extract.

# Merry garcia ice cream

SERVES 4

100g (⅔ cup) cashews, soaked overnight or a minimum of 3 hours, then rinsed and drained

3 Medjool dates, pitted and soaked for 10 minutes in hot water, then drained

Juice of ½ a lemon

1 x 400ml tin full-fat coconut milk

2 tsp vanilla extract or 1 vanilla pod

50ml amaretto

3 tbsp maple syrup

2 tbsp coconut oil, melted

200g pitted cherries, halved

150g vegan dark chocolate, cut into chunks

Put the cashews, dates, lemon juice, coconut milk, vanilla, amaretto and maple syrup into a blender. Blend for 3-5 minutes, or until the mixture is completely smooth and silky. Taste and add more maple syrup if you want it sweeter. Add the melted coconut oil to the mixture and pulse for another 30 seconds to blend it in. Pour into a freezerproof container, cover with a lid and freeze for 5 hours.

Remove and leave to soften for 30 minutes, then blend with a stick blender until smooth.

Add in the halved pitted cherries, dark chocolate chunks and mix, then return to the container, seal and return to the freezer for another 5 hours.

Remove from the freezer 10 minutes before serving to allow it soften, then scoop into bowls.

Treats

# Index

Index

**BRETT COBLEY** is a believer that good food and open conversation can change the world. In March 2016, after watching *101 Reasons to Go Vegan*, he made the decision to go vegan overnight. Shortly afterwards he set up the @epivegan Instagram account and later started a YouTube channel, making recipe videos and conducting interviews while cooking for his guests. Unsure of how to approach a fully vegan diet, and what foods he could and couldn't eat, Brett spent the first few weeks eating pretty much only veg, fruit and nuts! However, having always been passionate about cooking and eating, especially with friends and family, he made it his mission to veganise all his favourite meals and share them with the world, developing creative, delicious and comforting dishes to show that a vegan lifestyle is inclusive, simple and full of flavour, and so his first cookbook, *What Vegans Eat*, was born!